THE SAGA OF SUDDEN SAM

THE RISE, FALL, AND REDEMPTION OF SAM MCDOWELL

Sam McDowell
With Martin Gitlin

ROWMAN & LITTLEFIELD
Lanham • Boulder • New York • London

Published by Rowman & Littlefield
An imprint of The Rowman & Littlefield Publishing Group, Inc.
4501 Forbes Boulevard, Suite 200, Lanham, Maryland 20706
www.rowman.com

86-90 Paul Street, London EC2A 4NE, United Kingdom

British Library Cataloguing in Publication Information Available

Library of Congress Cataloging-in-Publication Data
Names: McDowell, Sam, 1942–author. | Gitlin, Marty, author.
Title: The saga of Sudden Sam : the rise, fall, and redemption of Sam McDowell /
    Sam McDowell, with Martin Gitlin.
Description: Lanham : Rowman & Littlefield, [2022] | Includes index. | Summary:
    "The candid autobiography of all-star pitcher "Sudden Sam" McDowell, whose
    alcohol-fueled life quickly and famously spiraled out of control, and his ultimate
    redemption as a counselor for other athletes suffering from addiction"— Provided
    by publisher.
Identifiers: LCCN 2021027479 (print) | LCCN 2021027480 (ebook) |
    ISBN 9781538156414 (Cloth : acid-free paper) | ISBN 9781538199053
    (Paperback : acid-free paper) | ISBN 9781538156421 (ePub)
Subjects: LCSH: McDowell, Sam, 1942- | Pitchers (Baseball)—United States—
    Biography. | Baseball players—United States—Biography. | Cleveland Indians
    (Baseball team)—History. | Major League Baseball (Organization)—History. |
    Alcoholics—Rehabilitation—United States—Biography. | Addicts—Family
    relationships. | Self-actualization (Psychology)
Classification: LCC GV865.M2935 A3 2022 (print) | LCC GV865.M2935 (ebook) |
    DDC 796.357092 [B]—dc23
LC record available at https://lccn.loc.gov/2021027479
LC ebook record available at https://lccn.loc.gov/2021027480

I would like to dedicate this book to my two children, who went through Hell and back with me; my former wife, who saved my children; my current wife, who is always there with her patience and understanding; and my parents, who never gave up on me or let up with their love and serious pressure on me for my recovery. There are so many individuals who help an alcoholic or drug addict during his or her recovery. I am no different and would like to acknowledge my mentor Dr. Abraham Twerski, Bob Case, Bill Nixon, Father Murry, and the numerous professors at Pitt and Duquesne University who gave me help and understanding, many of whom are still involved in recovery more than forty years later. And finally, yes, I would like to thank every single individual I ever worked with not mentioned here who helped me and my recovery!

—Sam McDowell

For my father, who turned me on to baseball as a young child. I am forever indebted to him for that.

—Martin Gitlin

CONTENTS

FOREWORD

Once in a while a sport produces a larger-than-life performer, that can't-miss athlete who seems destined for greatness. And sometimes that expectation becomes as much a burden as it does a virtue.

Standing 6 foot 5 inches, with an intimidating fastball and knee-buckling curve, Sam McDowell had a piercing look that had the batter behind 0-2 in the count before he even threw a pitch. I know because I faced him. It was never a comfortable at-bat. It was high anxiety because of that 100 mph fastball that wasn't always in the strike zone. You see, Sam was erratic enough to win twenty games and lead the league in strikeouts five times but also to lead the league in walks and wild pitches!

Sudden Sam was expected to be a Hall of Famer like Sandy Koufax or Don Drysdale, even Bob Gibson or Juan Marichal. It turned out he was a very good Sam McDowell, but that was better than 90 percent of the pitchers of his era.

The challenge of potential is that it is usually most celebrated by those who are invested in judging talent. They do not have to perform. They have no responsibility for failure or to live up to levels reached by only a few in history. In Sam's case, trying to live up to the expectations of others led to mental strain and a pressure to perform that was beyond reality. With these demands came fragility and insecurity, and that led to the need to escape.

Sam succumbed to depression and addiction, those two dreaded impostors that drain the life and career of a good man. It was a steep fall, and then a long climb back, but he had that deep-down soulful strength that takes courage—the courage to ask for help, to trust in others, and to realize you have a problem.

My favorite saying is "Life is God's gift to us; what we do with it is our gift to God." Sam fought his way back to being a voice for not giving up and for giving back. By sharing his life with those who might relate to it, and by successfully using tools similar to the ones that made him a star on the field, Sam McDowell has lived a life well worth living.

—Steve Garvey

1

A GUN TO MY HEAD

I was gripped by a sense of hopelessness. So I gripped my chrome-plated .38-caliber revolver. Then I placed it to my head. I had concluded that suicide was the only escape from my despair.

The date of my attempt to blow my brains out remains as hazy as the alcoholic fog that controlled my life for years. This chilling moment occurred in the chilly winter after a 1963 baseball season during which I experienced my first bouts with drunkenness and continued failures on the mound as a prized pitching prospect for the Cleveland Indians. My wife Carol Ann had left me and taken our baby daughter Debbie with her. I could not live like that so I decided to die.

My self-absorbed personality would not allow me to consider the consequences. I never reflected upon the anguish my death would have brought my family, friends, and fans. I did not realize that addiction is a disease of escapism that negatively affects the part of the brain that deals with fear, logic, decision making, and chance taking. Feelings of loneliness and misery perpetuated by what I perceived as abandonment by Carol rather than a departure justified by my behavior sent dangerous ideas swirling through my mind. So I pulled the trigger.

Nothing.

In loading the gun after cleaning it, I had unknowingly inserted a dead shell along with live loads. The gun clicked on the dead shell and never fired. I cashed in on a 17 percent survival rate. To this day I do not know why I did not try again. Perhaps my will to live proved stronger than my desire to perish. Perhaps the attempt to take my life was so traumatic that it scared me straight. I recall a vague sense that maybe I could figure out the problem. I believed it just enough to not try again. I just sat there in amazement, stunned. The introspection began. I remember thinking that I could not even do *this* right.

Whatever the reason, I am today very thankful that fate stepped in. The cost of my ignorance and immaturity was my marriage, career, and years of depression that I could not even identify as depression. But decades after my suicide attempt I finally gained self-actualization that brought happiness and contentment into my life. And I understood the disease that motivated me to try to end my life.

I would not have been alone and miserable that day had I heeded the warnings from Carol Ann, who was, along with her parents, a non-drinker. She had grown wary of my drinking and verbal abuse even though neither had become pronounced. I was only a periodic drinker at that time though I must admit I usually drank to get drunk. Not until the early 1970s did I deteriorate into what I identified many years later as the worst drunk in baseball. I never physically harmed her, though not treating her like a queen as she deserved I would call a form of mistreatment.

But I did not care when she spoke about a relative whose alcoholism and cruelty as a husband put fear in her own heart and mind about me. I did not listen when she questioned my desire to booze it up with neighbors and return a bit more than tipsy. I did not show any tenderness and compassion when she worried aloud about the dynamic of having a professional athlete on the road constantly as a life partner. And I did not try to recognize her overwhelming task as mother, father, mentor, teacher, provider, and disciplinarian before trying in vain to turn some of those roles over to a narcissist like me during the winter. I lived the creed "What I Want, When I Want, How I Want." That would eventually apply to my intoxicated trysts with other women.

Instead of seeking to understand her anxieties, I rebelled against them. I convinced myself that her concerns about me deteriorating into someone like her alcoholic relative were pure paranoia. My irrational thoughts turned into action. I persuaded myself that she had left me unduly and that my misery was inescapable. I could no longer fight it.

I was wrong, of course. I needed to show Carol Ann love. But in addicts there is no capacity for true, genuine love. They do not understand it. They are consumed by personal, base desires. I had been as contented as an alcoholic could be with the high school sweetheart who had become my wife and mother of my child. Fortunately God protected them because I could not do so, at least emotionally. To have what most people dream about—a home, family, and athletic career—and destroy it all? That is alcoholism.

The ultimate deed against myself occurred three days after Carol Ann had packed her bags and bolted to the Pittsburgh home of her parents. I had come home drunk on a couple occasions and she felt that her fears were being realized. Her departure made me feel for the first time in my life that something was wrong. That recognition mushroomed in my head to a belief that all hope was lost. I angrily thought, "What's so bad about getting drunk once in a while? Why does my wife not understand me? I'm only drinking once or twice a month." There was no way out but leaving this earth. Carol Ann must have had an inkling that I might do something desperate because she asked a neighbor to come over and check up on me. I had yet to attempt the suicide but it must have been at least a bit frightening when my neighbor arrived to find me cleaning all my guns.

I had an impressive collection that included handguns, rifles, and one shotgun. I had begun to purchase firearms in spring training 1963 when my teammate and future Indians manager Joe Adcock asked me to accompany him on a coyote hunt. I immediately bought a rifle and bullets to go along with western boots. We only hunted twice during that camp but for the next eight springs I arrived early in Tucson to hunt and drink. I then started to hunt in my native Pennsylvania during the offseason and bought a 30/30 rifle for heavily wooded areas as opposed to the wide-open spaces of Arizona. I later began accumulating specialty, collector guns. But it is interesting that as I started to recover from my alcoholism and depression I no longer felt the desire to hunt. I even gave away or sold my guns, though I must admit that before my emotional breakthrough I had hawked guns to get money to pay for booze.

My alcoholism during the winter in which I attempted suicide had not advanced enough for me to understand it as alcoholism. That was not the only problem with which I was afflicted that I did not comprehend—though they were all tied together. Another was depression. It is hard to imagine, given that I had just placed a gun to my head and pulled the trigger, that I did not realize I suffered from clinical depression.

You have to consider the times. Such a term, "depression," did not exist then especially in the athletic arena. The number of athletes who realized they were depressed and admitted it publicly could be found by looking in the middle of a doughnut. Back then, depression and other mental or emotional disorders were not openly discussed. Addiction was also considered a mental illness until the 1970s when research proved it to be a disease. Such issues are more openly examined today—athletes have revealed their personal battle against depression in recent years. But even today most people, including athletes, continue to hide it. And they believe there is no light at the end of the tunnel, not realizing there is a solution. That is why the suicide rate remains tragically high.

One problem with which I am painfully familiar and that certainly played a role in preventing me from finding and getting help for my alcoholism and depression in the early 1960s was that families rarely intervened to that extent. The only solution embraced by society years ago was to see a psychiatrist. That is what my boss in the insurance industry after my retirement from baseball suggested. Nobody urged me to check into a rehabilitation center because they did not know of any. And many of those who contemplated or attempted suicide felt too ashamed or frightened to share the experience with loved ones. I did not tell anyone about my own attempt until I informed Carol Ann years later.

My parents and siblings simply implored me to "get help." They never offered where to get that help. They complained that I was a drunk, and I hated that word. I despised it because it inspired thoughts within me that I might indeed have a drinking problem. I did not want to think about that. I preferred to see myself as living an accepted celebrity lifestyle. I would convince myself that I was fine by regaling my inner thoughts with stories about the legendary Babe Ruth and other sports superstars and their drunken escapades. Among those whose alcoholism famously became public knowledge was Mickey Mantle, another immortal Yankees slugger and my hero during my playing days. Little could I have imagined when I was going *mano y mano* against Mantle on American League mounds that he would eventually admit that alcoholism had destroyed his life. He died tragically young at sixty-three, though it must be cited that he passed away sober, back with his family and loving wife.

I had yet to begin binge drinking during the winter of 1963. I would get drunk maybe two or three times a month. But that was enough, given the fears of Carol Ann, to threaten our marriage as well as friendships and other relationships. Everyone—not just my wife, parents, and siblings—began confronting me about my drinking. After my bouts with booze I would make promises to Carol Ann that I was incapable of keeping. I took steps to placate her and followed through but they proved worthless because I had not come to grips with my real problems—narcissism, addiction, and depression (which is a part of addiction and not a separate malady like clinical depression). I simply did not understand why I could not take a social drink and stop before reaching the point of drunkenness. I then promised myself that the next time I would stop before getting drunk. It did not happen. Not only did I fail to stop drinking in excess, I began boozing more often. Since I did not get inebriated on every occasion, I fooled myself into thinking I was a simply a social drinker.

One of my attempts at sobriety involved sports psychology. I had befriended the director of the Psychology Department at Duquesne University and my former Catholic parish priest who expressed a desire and willingness to help me. One of the interesting aspects of my vain efforts was that I carried out my mission without telling Carol Ann. Logically one would think I would want her to know that I was working to improve myself.

My personality disorders, including denial, prevented me from admitting to others that I had a problem. Because of the prevailing thoughts on addiction, I did not want anyone to think I was weak or had a mental illness. So I carried out my mission without informing any friends or family members. I told my wife that I had to attend a banquet or made up some other appointment before visiting the psychologist or priest—and of course have a few drinks on the way home. But I requested from them that we focus on sports psychology as I had convinced myself that was my issue.

We didn't delve into alcoholism. I took courses in sports psychology that I later learned were all theoretical, not applied. I read books on the subject. I would purchase and listen repeatedly to motivational tapes, particularly during road trips. Though I refused to admit it to those close to me, I knew there was something wrong. But I convinced myself that it could not be addiction. My research into sports psychology and denial of my real problems continued for years. My baseball colleagues scoffed at me for delving into the subject. I recall one teammate and roommate making fun of me after he had been drinking for reading a book on sports psychology. He badgered me about it for several days.

Indians coach Kerby Farrell—a nice man with whom I had deep philosophical differences as time passed about how to maximize my effectiveness as a pitcher—also chastised me. On one occasion as I listened to a tape on sports psychology, he exclaimed, "You don't need that shit; just listen to me." He stayed on my case constantly. Another of our coaches, Joe Lutz, who had studied psychology and loved it and whose locker was near mine, enjoyed sitting and hearing some of my tapes. When Farrell saw him listening with me, he chewed Joe's ass out so loudly that all of us could hear.

Sports psychology helped me but only professionally. My exploration sharpened my focus and concentration while helping me relax on the mound. It also helped me get rid of fears, transforming me into an aggressive, positive pitcher instead of a defensive one. The problem was it would not stick and periodically I would forget it and have to begin all over again. My addiction played a significant role in these breakdowns. But sports psychology eventually aided me in my future work as a counselor.

There came a point during my baseball career when I knew deep down that something was still wrong, and I eventually turned into an angry drunk who engaged in barroom brawls and landed in jail. But it was not until five years after I had drunk myself out of baseball that I began to learn that only an education in addiction and depression rather than sports psychology would allow me to forge a path to happiness and fulfillment.

My budding addiction had not yet destroyed my life that fateful winter of 1963. But the fog I was living in perpetuated by my alcoholic personality and coupled with the miserable reality of my wife leaving me was wrecking everything. Fortunately, Carol Ann returned to me then as she did on several other occasions after she'd bolted, having been overwhelmed every time by my inability to feel genuine love and unwillingness to provide emotional support. I would feel more secure when she came back but could not change my behavior. I was simply incapable of this until I gained an education in the 1980s that allowed me to learn about and rid myself of my disease.

It all seems so strange looking back on my career. Even though I was doing nothing to improve myself as a person and was actually descending deeper and deeper into depression, alcoholism, and depravity, I thought constantly about Carol Ann, Debbie, and my son Tim (who was born in August 1965). When the team was on the road I called home every night to talk to all of them. That would have made most individuals feel good about their marriage. But I would immediately start blaming Carol Ann in my mind for what I perceived as her misunderstanding me.

I do not want to give the impression that I had bad intentions as a husband and father or that I provided nothing but my earnings to the household. My obsessive-compulsive disorder made me a control freak and I had no clue about how to be a husband and father. I truly believed that taking care of the finances and tinkering around the house made me a good husband and that Carol Ann should be responsible for cooking and cleaning and for nurturing the children. This was very old-school—I was mimicking my father. So I was strict with the kids. If my angry voice did not inspire the right reaction from my children I resorted to spanking. That, however, was rare. I can vaguely recall doing this once or twice.

My relationship to my children had of course evolved by the late 1960s and early 1970s as my alcoholism became more pronounced and forced me to wind down my baseball career. There was no disciplining necessary before Tim was born and Debbie was still an infant. Between the periods when an angry and frustrated Carol Ann left me, I felt contented just knowing she was there. I made myself believe that I was loving my family the best I could. And given my narcissism coupled with my alcoholic personality, I suppose I did. That is why I felt so trapped during the winter of my discontent. It had finally dawned on me that something was wrong and my disorders would not allow me to blame myself. My mind told me there was no escape but suicide.

I was a creature of habit, and Carol Ann's departures made me feel like my entire universe had been thrown off course. Suddenly I felt a profound sense of emptiness. When Carol Ann was with me, everything seemed complete. I had little to think about or do. She took care of me at home and the team took care of me during spring training and the regular season at Cleveland Stadium and on the road. I even had an offseason job working in the sporting goods department at Gimbels, a major retail department store, even though the family was capable of stretching my baseball salary year-round. Every so often I would stop at a neighborhood bar with my coworkers to down some beers. Then during the season I began drinking more on the road. I did not booze it up often but when I did I often could not stop until I was plastered.

And I did not care. I had convinced myself that I was simply embracing a celebrity lifestyle. And being drunk brought me a sense of normalcy and social confidence that I did not feel when I was sober. Eventually my drunkenness became so frequent and out of control that it resulted in massive instability in my personal and professional life. That was dangerous for someone such as me who required a stable existence. But I could not stop. I was an alcoholic.

It was too bad I could not revert to my mindless periodic drinking days of the early 1960s. I had at that time a comfort level that did not require me to think much. That was the mindset I needed. Any deep thought into my narcissistic motivations would have resulted in turmoil. I was simply too ignorant and immature to turn such realizations into positive changes as a person. In some ways I was still the same joyless, robotic child growing up in Pittsburgh who could not recognize his negative personality traits or summon any enthusiasm for the career path his talents demanded.

2

THE MELANCHOLY
CHILD

If only modern me the counselor could accompany a child psychologist into a time machine and travel back seven decades to explore the feelings and motivations of childhood Sam. I can just imagine the pain and suffering that could have been avoided in later years.

What we would see would be a joyless boy. I never felt loved. My achievements went unpraised but I could not recognize that my parents refused to praise me. I did not know I was experiencing an unhappy childhood because happiness was a foreign concept to me. I cannot say I was either happy or sad. I did not even understand I was depressed as it was my constant state to which I had nothing to compare.

But I was always in some form of depression. I did not react to humor that inspired laughter from others. I did not see the beauty in things that most people did. I simply plodded along as the black sheep of the family. I craved attention and acted out in negative ways to get it. I was generally in trouble, trying to get away with bad behavior, always going against the grain, displaying a genetically infused alcoholic personality that I would not grasp until well after my baseball career.

The seeds had long been planted. The mixture was one part narcissism, one part depression, one part low self-esteem. This reality remained far beyond my comprehension for decades and negatively affected all aspects of my personal and professional life until my recovery began and continuing education led to enlightenment.

The difference between right and wrong escaped me as a child. Only a lack of motivation toward illegal or dangerous activities rather than any sense of honesty or morality prevented me from engaging in petty theft or bullying. But I was dishonest. I would lie about anything, spewing out even the most insignificant claims. And I certainly misbehaved. I rebelled against my parents. They would warn me not to leave the house or befriend those they considered undesirable characters and I would leave the house and befriend those undesirable characters. I spent money from my paper route that was supposed to be paid on Saturdays, forcing my mother to take the funds from the family pot. Rather than turn in the payments, I would then stop at a wonderful Italian delicatessen and use the money to buy cream puffs and candy. I would also tell neighbors on my route that I was going away for a week or more so they needed to pay me for their papers in advance.

My disobeying often resulted in a spanking or paddling, but I remained undeterred. No discipline meted out by my parents directed me toward the straight and narrow. I was unknowingly following the narcissist creed "What I Want, When I Want, How I Want."

And to Hell with good versus evil, a notion one would assume had been drilled into me growing up in a strongly Catholic home. Any positive effects derived from religious teaching were more than negated by living within a highly dysfunctional family that engendered little affection from parent to child or sibling to sibling.

Only through a lesson in genealogy could I recognize the stifling negativity that permeated the McDowell household despite the many positive qualities exhibited by Mom and Dad. My parents and grandparents were born and raised in the United States. My father's side of the family had Irish roots; my mother's ancestors were Scottish. Both my parents were alcoholics though my mother hid her drinking well as a response to menopause. Her addiction became obvious only later in life.

I had no knowledge as a kid how their experiences as young adults that shattered their career aspirations negatively affected their parenting. I cannot blame myself for that—most children are far too needy and self-centered to care about things like that. And they are certainly not advanced enough intellectually to understand how the experiences of their parents alter their mental and emotional states.

Fate had dashed the hopes and dreams of Tom and MaryIrene McDowell. My dad, who came from a stable family, played quarterback for a University of Pittsburgh team that qualified for the Rose Bowl. During his college years he toiled as a part-time salesman for Firestone, which served as a local supplier for the Pittsburgh area. He not only boasted a background in engineering but was pursuing a career in dentistry when World War II interrupted his studies.

Though his marital status with one child precluded him from being drafted, his education resulted in a request to monitor magnetism in the steel plates being produced because the Japanese were planting magnetic mines that were blowing up American ships in the Pacific. His work there ended his dentistry career. He continued toiling in steel mills for more than three decades.

My mother was the product of a wealthy family. She had lofty goals as a budding concert pianist while studying at the University of Cincinnati Conservatory of Music. But she settled into married life and motherhood. Her upbringing in a well-to-do setting headed by a father who owned stockyards near Pittsburgh that supplied the entire tri-state area made her detest any reference to our own family neighborhood as part of the lower economic strata of the city. None of us kids ever really wanted for things others may have had such as bicycles, fancy clothes, spending money, watches, and jewelry. We were all were so busy with sports we didn't have time for that stuff. We always had food, clothing, a roof over our head and parents who cared about everything we were doing.

That my parents showed no affection toward their children was as much a reflection of the times as it was a reflection of character. Their philosophy was that praise weakened rather than strengthened offspring. The result for me was a feeling that it was impossible to please them so why try by behaving well? They provided no warmth, no comfort, no compliments, no acknowledgment of a job well done. I will never forget pitching a no-hitter in Little League and my father refusing to stop on the way home for a celebratory ice cream treat, instead criticizing me all the way back for perceived mistakes I had made during the game.

Only through the admiration of his old high school football teammates during a luncheon decades later did my dad finally show me even the slightest appreciation. After a local newspaper told the story of my recovery from alcohol addiction and his gridiron buddies at a high school reunion expressed pride to me about the enormous obstacles I had overcome, he shook my hand and tearfully acknowledged that he too was proud. It would be the last time he praised me. And though I took pleasure in that one fleeting moment, I realized that it was far too little, far too late. Many parents back then didn't praise, but we all knew they cared. In fact if anyone saw a parent kissing or hugging their child, we'd make fun of that boy or girl. We'd call them a "sissy" or a "mama's boy."

Some might speculate that my parents grew bitter when their career ambitions never materialized but I can neither accept nor deny that. The financial and personal responsibilities of raising a family certainly became a priority. They not only brought up six kids but took in my grandfather and uncle to live with us. My father was employed at the Homestead steel mill, the largest of many that kept Pittsburgh humming during and after the war. I recall the hardships my parents endured during worker strikes that left them scrambling for enough money to pay the bills. The free powdered milk, cheese, and stale bread the union supplied the households of strikers did not keep a family of ten well fed.

The work stoppages took a financial toll on all of us and an emotional toll on my dad. He became angry that they resulted in only a small bump in pay. He railed against what he perceived as a lack of employee power compared to the union bigwigs who demanded strikes. My dad told us stories of serious intimidation as well as physical damage done to any worker or family member who went against union wishes. On one occasion my dad went to Pittsburgh Hospital to visit a friend and colleague who had been beaten severely because he dared to make a statement about family conditions without a paycheck. The workers ultimately gained a decent wage from their persistence, but my father and his colleagues went through Hell getting there.

That pressure contributed to his alcoholic binges. He did not take a social drink or two. When he would drink he usually got drunk, be it accidentally or intentionally, a practice with which I became personally familiar as a young adult and beyond. He did not booze it up on a regular basis. But when he did at a party or during a stop at a bar after work, he gulped down enough to get snockered.

Yet despite his issues that I became painfully aware of, I yearned throughout my childhood to follow in his footsteps. I felt an admiration for the positive contributions my father made to the family and not simply to our pursuits of athletic excellence. I recall vividly his ability to assemble television sets or radios from scratch. He even used his wiring talents to build a heater that warmed the family during those chilly Pittsburgh winters. He remodeled our bedroom and bathroom and constructed a backboard and basketball hoop that he attached to the disconnected garage. Though never formally trained in wiring, plumbing, carpentry, cement work, or refinishing furniture, he was amazing. He read books from the library or manuals, picked up parts others threw away or from the junkyard to bring home, and eventually you'd see a finished product you would swear came from a furniture or electronic or appliance store. No automobile would break down that he could not fix. It was not all about saving money. He enjoyed making things. I used to watch him wiring or plumbing and he would explain what he was doing, what an alternating current was, what a short was, what direct current was, why he was using copper wire or copper pipes, and how to solder joints so they would not leak.

His influence on my career in sports cannot be overstated. My passions were not limited to baseball, football, and basketball. I even became quite proficient in tennis after befriending the children of a local psychiatrist who worked at the University of Pittsburgh Medical Center and competing against them with an old wooden racket I found in our attic.

Fortunately for the sake of the family my mother's alcoholism did not become pronounced until after menopause. Though my mom, like her husband, did not embrace the necessity of displaying love and affection as a parent, she did dedicate herself to the basic financial and physical well-being of her family. She meticulously cut out coupons to save money on food and clothing. Rather than spend on new clothes for her sons she insisted that we all wear hand-me-downs from an elder sibling. My mother would go food shopping every Saturday, prepare a wonderful Sunday dinner, then spread out the leftovers to make casseroles and create meals for the rest of the week. Her expertise and influence in food preparation remains with me to this day—I still love leftovers. She insisted on preparing healthful fare or at least what was considered well-balanced in the 1940s and 1950s. We always had starches and vegetables, as well as a meat, except on Fridays. She was a true matriarch. She controlled the finances judiciously enough to allow her family to make ends meet.

And though neither of my parents showed love, my mother did drill into me a need to perform well in the classroom. The notion certainly clashed with my penchant for bad behavior early in my life. I battled against it with all my will. When she started insisting we sit down after dinner so she could help me with my homework, I rebelled by claiming I had none or by intentionally failing to bring my books home from school. So she hit back where it hurt the most. Knowing my love for participating in baseball, football, basketball, and cross country, she ruled that I could not play any organized sports unless I earned all As and Bs on my report card. Her strategy worked so well that she upped the ante a year later by banning all sports activity unless I received nothing but As. I did just that over my last two years of high school. I did not find acing all my classes particularly difficult.

While most of my classmates often skipped school to hang out somewhere around town, I dutifully attended daily, even if I was sick. My motivation was not necessarily academic. I realize looking back that I felt I would garner more of the attention I craved in school rather than away from it. It was not a perfect outlook but it certainly helped me blossom into an excellent student.

My mother was a devout Roman Catholic who indoctrinated my father in the same religious beliefs before they married. Both tried to keep me on the straight and narrow through religion. We attended mass every Sunday and holy day without exception. It did not matter if Mother Nature threw all her fury at Pittsburgh in the winter. Even if we could not escape the snow in our driveway, we followed the streetcar tracks by foot and rode it to church. I served as an altar boy along with my brothers through high school and even during my first two years of professional baseball. I even served the same role at my sister's wedding during my second year in professional baseball.

Neither of my parents helped foster positive sibling relationships, though I wonder if that could even be achieved given our competitive personalities. My relationships with my four brothers—one older and three younger—were not ideal. We were all accomplished, talented athletes. But there was no healthy competition among us. Rivalries resulted in harmful jealousies. I was not the only one adversely affected. And none of my siblings' athletic pursuits had a happy ending. Though I was considered perhaps the finest baseball prospect in the country when I reached my senior season at Central Catholic High School, I can state unequivocally that my older brother Tom Jr. was a more talented pitcher. He also excelled in football. But all his college scholarship offers were withdrawn when he contracted polio. The football aspirations of my younger brother Warren, whom we called Butch, were destroyed when he broke his arm on a rushing attempt during a college game. And my youngest brother Donny proved simply too lazy and stubborn to maximize his vast athletic talents.

We were lucky as kids in regard to sports. The school playgrounds for which the Pittsburgh Parks and Recreation Department provided a variety of activities were right across the street. We played baseball in a fenced-in area and basketball on the hard court. Tom—five years my senior—emerged as a brilliant athlete. He excelled with a sandlot baseball team managed by my father, who even let little eight-year-old Sam wear a uniform and sit on the bench. We all got our exercise even before and after the game, trekking five miles up and down a steep hill to the Caddy Grounds park.

That is where I displayed the first spark of baseball talent, bolstered by competing with and against older kids. Even though I nearly exclusively had my butt planted on the pine during games, my father allowed me to practice with the team. But one day he surprised everyone by summoning me to play center field. He figured it would give me confidence and that our six-run lead was safe enough—I could not do much damage. I not only avoided disaster, I helped preserve the advantage. I fielded a one-hop single that bounced my way and heaved a throw to home plate that nailed a runner trying to score.

This shocking display of arm strength for a kid five years younger than his teammates was a wake-up call to my dad. He began grooming me as a pitcher. His knowledge and background in engineering came in handy as he constructed my windup and delivery. He taught me how to throw a fastball and curve using lessons about the different muscle groups in my back and arm and illustrating what was required of me to maximize the effect on the ball. People have asked me how I could have developed so many pitches to a major league level before I'd ever played professionally. It was mostly because my father explained to me how my arm was supposed to move for each pitch and how the muscles worked to make the pitch work. He used the same technical knowledge to teach my brother Tom how to create a spiral on the football to maximize distance as a punter.

Neither of my parents worked to bolster my sagging self-image, though in their defense they were not aware of it or trained to do so if they had been. But they certainly put time and effort into preparing us for the future athletically, academically, and morally. My father toiled so tirelessly it is a wonder he ever slept. He worked a rotating shift of mornings, afternoons, and nights at the steel mill. He ran errands for his wife. And he still found time to share his expertise in athletics with his sons. Some parents who excel in sports—such as my dad, who not only played quarterback at Pitt but performed well as an amateur baseball player—burn out and do not pass their expertise to their offspring. My father did so willingly and enthusiastically.

Our family eventually moved to Highland Park, which was located across a great ravine known as Morningside and a bit closer to the Caddy Grounds. At age twelve my parents enrolled me in a Little League system that played its games about five miles from our new home. I again was forced to trek there and back—with six children in the family I could only hope to be lucky enough that my parents would drive me to practices and games. But they were often hauling one of my siblings somewhere.

Our Morningside team, for which I pitched and played shortstop, was a powerhouse. We captured so many championships around town that we were invited to Williamsport to compete in the Little League World Series. We featured many fine athletes—it still amazes me, having witnessed their talent firsthand through high school, that I was the only one who emerged as a professional ballplayer. Our team fell in the second round.

It is a shame as I look back at my childhood that I was incapable of feeling a sense of joy over my accomplishments for I certainly racked up many during my Little League days. One inducement aside from personal satisfaction was an offer from a pharmacy located right next to the field of a free pint of ice cream to any player who hit a home run or pitched a no-hitter. I hurled three no-hitters that year but only cashed in on two containers of that yummy treat. My father forbade me from grabbing my prize after one of those mound masterpieces. That was the time he claimed I'd made too many mistakes in the game to be deserving. I was upset over his refusal to allow me to pick up the ice cream I believed I had earned, but my dad was an extremely headstrong person. What he proclaimed could not be disputed.

Unlike many kids of the modern era who focus on one sport, those in my day played several even if they realized that they only excelled in one. I remained undiscouraged as I occupied the bench during my first season of grade-school basketball. I improved my skill level to land a starting spot the following year and found my niche on the gridiron as well, moving from wide receiver to quarterback. But by the time I entered high school it had become obvious that my greatest athletic talent was as a baseball pitcher. I would eventually become the most sought-after prospect in America, a distinction for which I was ready neither mentally nor emotionally.

Nothing I achieved positively affected my self-esteem or brought me pleasure. Never mind all the no-hitters. Never mind the praise from the media, which began to take notice of my talent. Never mind the scouts buzzing around me. It was not only that my success on the mound failed to bolster the image I had of myself. I *had* no image of myself. I was emotionally numb, even while pitching. I performed robotically. That was bad enough. My alcoholic personality eventually placed me in more dire circumstances. But nobody among the students at Central Catholic High School or those who followed the exploits of the baseball team, least of all me, grasped the dangers of my emotional state. They were too busy fawning over my mastery on the mound, which soon became known far beyond western Pennsylvania.

I attended the same high school as Hall of Fame quarterback Dan Marino. Pittsburgh and its surrounding area became legendary for producing premier sports standouts, including football stars Mike Ditka and Joe Namath and baseball slugger Dick Allen. During the 1950s, 1960s, and 1970s, over sixty professional athletes came out of the area. Pittsburgh remains a hotbed for baseball players despite their inability to play during the winter as do prospects in California and Florida. But none has ever left the area with greater notoriety than Sam McDowell.

3

UNRECOGNIZED
GREATNESS

It seems ridiculous for me to state unambiguously that I had no idea through most of my high school years that I was destined for a baseball career. I tell that to folks and they look at me like I have ten ears. After all, I was dominating hitters as few prep pitchers ever had. And scouts were beginning to frequent my games in vast numbers. Yet I had no clue. Never in my wildest dreams did I imagine such a future for myself.

Two primary factors entered into the equation. One was that no level of success could have improved my self-image. From any rational, objective view, I could hardly have been more accomplished as a teenager. Not only had I emerged as the premier pitching prospect in the country and gained such notoriety that I was eventually invited to speak about my talents and announce my signing of a professional contract on national television, but I had blossomed academically into a straight-A student. Yet how does one define success? If it is finding a strong sense of pride and happiness, if it is gaining drive and determination while seeking a purpose in life and embracing a passion for a talent that could result in a career, I had fallen woefully short. It is not that my self-esteem was lacking. I had no self-esteem at all. I went through my daily routines on and off the field robotically. It was not a matter of misunderstanding the opportunity in front of me, the interest in me as a pitcher. It was that I never gave it any thought.

The other element was ignorance. It seems unbelievable to many people but I was greatly unaware of major league baseball through most of my childhood and adolescence. I never attended Pirates games. My initial experience with professional baseball was pitching my first game for Class D Lakeland. We did not have a television until I was in high school and beyond that I never watched a game or listened to one on the radio. With ten mouths to feed and bodies to clothe we did not have the money to attend ballgames. Nor did I have the time. I was always out playing at the amateur level or working at one of many jobs over the years, such as the paper route I inherited from my brother, cleaning out neighborhood cellars and garages, or toiling as a soda jerk and delivering prescriptions in an open Jeep after earning my driver's license. The sport of baseball outside of my world remained a mystery.

My coaches during my amateur career in Pittsburgh often urged me to display my talents at various training camps. But I generally refused. I neither cared about nor understood their importance. I did attend one and was sorry I did when a thrown ball smacked me in the right side of my skull and left an indentation the size of a silver dollar that I can still identify.

This lack of awareness of opportunities to further my career or even to forge one at all seems odd given the time and effort my father put into maximizing my talent. He did not focus specifically on me—he toiled ad nauseum on the football abilities of his namesake son, who eventually blossomed into a fine quarterback and the premier prep punter in Pittsburgh. But my dad worked tirelessly on my pitching mechanics. The two major newspapers became aware of my exploits on the mound, which in turn allowed the Pirates to take notice. They summoned me to pitch batting practice before games at Forbes Field, which was just two blocks from my high school. I believe now they patronized me so I would sign with them out of high school for less money (the amateur draft that evened the playing field and ended the bidding for high school and college talent had yet to become a reality).

It might have worked given my craving for attention. Most teenage prospects would have been wowed to be not only pitching batting practice to big leaguers but meeting many of the greats of their day. But I knew very little about those greats aside from faint recollections of hearing their names on the radio. I was not bowled over when I met stars of the Pirates and their rivals such as Ted Kluszewski, Stan Musial, Warren Spahn, Lew Burdette, even Hank Aaron. I did not even know who most of them were. The media made a big deal out of the fact that the immortal Roberto Clemente refused to get in the batter's box against me—I assume because he felt I was a bit too wild, though my control was fairly strong at that point in my career.

I spent time before batting practice in the Pirates locker room. The muscle-bound Kluszewski, who was fading as a player by that time, was always checking up on me, ensuring I was not overwhelmed. He had nothing to worry about. I remained my same mechanical self. One cold day I was sweating after batting practice at Forbes Field and a clubhouse worker gave me a jacket to keep me warm until I could shower and go home. He later returned to make certain I returned the jacket. I must admit I was seriously considering taking it. Though as a youth I generally stopped short of partaking in illegal activity, I was not against bending the rules to suit my desires.

Most significant about my experiences at Forbes Field is that nothing would have impacted me given the fog in which I was walking around. I had no realization of the honor or even the significance of a high school kid throwing batting practice to big leaguers, including those who played for one of the top teams in the National League and in a year or two would be beating the juggernaut Yankees in the World Series. I never even stuck around to watch the games to which I was invited. They began at 8 p.m., which would have allowed me to stay for several innings, but I could not have been less interested since it did not involve me. I viewed myself as a stagehand for the Pirates—just someone to set up the stage. Such a role meant nothing to this narcissist. Others my age would have given their two front teeth to be in my position. They would have been thrilled to have placed themselves on the precipice of greatness. I could not even work up a sense of excitement when I threw a no-hitter. I remained unaffected.

And if anyone should have been positively affected as an amateur player, it was me. I had emerged as the top pitcher on the Pittsburgh Central Catholic team as a junior. I went 8-0 my senior year without allowing an earned run and fanned practically every batter I retired—152 in 63 innings. I struck out 2.4 batters per inning, which is mind-boggling given that 1 per inning back in the late 1950s was considered dominant. I threw two no-hitters and one one-hitter to lead our team to the championship. I also played first base and even shortstop and hit well.

That same year I served as the ace of our team in the Colt League World Series in Pasadena, California. I had tossed mostly no-hitters and one-hitters to help us qualify for that prestigious event. I then crafted a one-hitter with twelve strikeouts in my only outing in the World Series. We lost our second game and returned home.

I certainly welcomed the competition and—of course as was typical of me—the attention. Very few schools were willing to play Central Catholic in football or baseball because of our dominance. We had to schedule outside the city to find teams brave or talented enough to compete against us. Our baseball team even scheduled the University of Pittsburgh in exhibitions. Among its best players was eventual NFL Hall of Fame tight end and coach Mike Ditka, who was also one hell of a baseball player.

I liked that games against top-caliber opponents in high school or the Colt League playoffs attracted a large number of fans. Local prep contests generally drew only the parents of players. But during our state championship run the stands were filled. I recall there were twenty-one scouts representing all sixteen major league teams for the title game. They were not all there to see me, but they certainly took notice when I pitched a no-hitter to outduel my talented rival Gary Wright. The only hit he allowed was my home run. I find it strange recollecting that I pitched in the Little League World Series, Pony League World Series, Colt League World Series and American Legion World Series yet never even sniffed the playoffs during a fifteen-year major league career.

It may also be hard to believe for many who know my story that through those early years I still did not foresee a future in baseball. It had become obvious for years that it was my best sport. I played defensive and offensive end and a little quarterback as a freshman and sophomore. I competed on my eighth-grade basketball team but was certainly no standout. I then played on the junior varsity and varsity teams, working my way up to first string and specializing in rebounding. (I had grown six inches so I certainly had the height for it.) But I had become such a dominant pitcher that the newspapers began printing articles about me and scouts started buzzing around.

Only then—only when the facts bludgeoned me over the head—did I finally gain some inkling that a career as a pitcher appeared inevitable. I should have gained that awareness years earlier. I earned a spot on the varsity baseball team as a freshman, which speaks volumes given the strength of the Central Catholic program. I pitched a no-hitter with fourteen strikeouts as a sophomore—against the University of Pittsburgh team, no less. The no-hitters the local media was marveling at piled up. Though my high school athletic director exaggerated the number, claiming to the newspapers that I had hurled fifteen no-hitters, I actually pitched nine. Yet I *still* did not grasp my greatness or understand my destiny until a professional baseball career was practically at my doorstep. That shows the depth of my immaturity and poor self-image as well as ignorance about the professional game. The emotional issues were part and parcel of what I learned later to be an "addictogenic" personality.

The reasons that enter into this contradiction are complex. They prevented me from reaching a healthy level of self-actualization until after I nearly destroyed my life. What I did not understand is that the self-esteem of most people is strengthened through accomplishment. But those with the personality traits common to alcoholics react neither positively nor negatively to achievement. I started hearing people talk about my "God-given talent" or "natural ability" as a pitcher. Rather than being perceived as a compliment, it prevented me from taking credit for my successes because I figured since I was born with such ability I had not really done anything. That proved exasperating throughout my career. I felt like nothing I achieved athletically could satisfy me—or anyone else for that matter.

What I learned nearly twenty-five years later to be an alcoholic personality adversely altered my personal life as well. Those with my disorder are narcissists who experience psychotic periods and are incapable of love in the proper sense. It is a form of obsessive-compulsive feeling. I could very strongly like somebody. I could want to be with that person and protect her. I could want her to idolize me. I could mouth the words, express love, because that's what I thought she wanted to hear. But I was incapable of feeling love or feeling loved.

All of which was a shame for the high school girlfriend who eventually became my wife. She attended a public school but I met through her two neighbors with whom I played sports. I sometimes visited Carol Ann and her sister and I would serve as a third wheel when we went out together. Her sister drove us all to the swimming pool and other destinations. For the first year of our relationship I did not consider Carol Ann my steady. I spent much time playing basketball or other games with her neighbors. Only later did I begin to date her as a girlfriend.

Carol Ann basically just put up with me. We lived five blocks apart and I was too busy with sports, particularly baseball, to spend an inordinate amount of time with her, plus I was holding down a job as a soda jerk. That was not the only kind of jerk I was as we became a couple. I often wondered in high school why I could not hang out with the boys more, an attitude that she felt shunned her. I was being pulled in many directions—baseball, school, work, girlfriend, boyfriends, family. It seemed I had no time for myself. I did not treat her well, especially after we wed. She was a perfect wife—beautiful inside and out, wonderful friend and lover, ideal mother, and mentor to the children. But the only love I could muster was for my obsessive-compulsive feelings and behavior. Love was like any other beauty in the world that I could not recognize or appreciate. It escaped me.

My immaturity negatively affected all aspects of my life mentally and emotionally. But it could not ruin the physical act of pitching. The fastball, curveball, slider, and change-up combination that super-slugger Reggie Jackson once called the best he had ever seen had already been established, though I did not often use them all in amateur competition. I threw hard but not nearly as fast as I did in the majors. I unleashed my curve from three different angles. I even delivered an occasional spitball. I only needed my fastball and curve to get batters out. And I knew pitchers in Pittsburgh alone who threw harder than me, including my teammate Bob Gordon, who also signed with the Indians, as well as Wright, who surprised me by not landing a professional contract.

What all the success in amateur ball, as well as the repetition and training with my father, did not instill in me was a productive mental approach to pitching. That made me wholly unprepared for the challenges of professional baseball. My talent alone overwhelmed batters in little league and high school. I did not have to consider pitch sequence or location. I was lost when it became apparent early in my career in the minors and majors that I could not simply blow fastballs by batters at that level. That tough discovery took a toll on me. I did not boast the maturity to deal with it, to channel the challenges to a positive direction.

Remember that the 1950s was not exactly an era of keen awareness regarding body and soul. Few amateur or even professional athletes worked to maximize wellness physically, mentally, or emotionally. One example is that the dangers of smoking cigarettes had yet to be proven—the evidence, though suspected, was not cemented and released until the early 1960s. I began smoking at age sixteen. I got cigarettes from the father of former major league pitcher Mel Queen, who served as a youth baseball volunteer and raised a son who enjoyed a productive career as a starter and reliever. I also stole cigarettes from my mother and father and snuck out to the backyard or a wooded area behind the garage to smoke them.

The smoking habit that remained with me, even after I had beaten alcohol and turned my life around, had no real impact on my pitching. At age sixteen I would not have known that danger anyway. I never considered a baseball career to be on the horizon.

4

THE BATTLE FOR SAM MCDOWELL AND BEYOND

It was as if someone had to bludgeon me over the head with a bat to make me realize that I had pitched my way into a baseball career. Not until scouts began offering gobs of money did I finally understand. Yet I still did not grasp the importance of what was happening to me. I did not comprehend the significance of making decisions that would affect the rest of my life.

My parents were protective. They wanted me to make the best choice but my father believed I would require as much coaching as possible. That is why one of his demands of all organizations was that I be placed at the lowest rung of the minor leagues upon signing a professional contract. I am not certain that stipulation was made because he recognized my immaturity or if he simply wanted me to take a path through the system similar to that of other players despite my status as arguably the premier prospect in the sport at that time.

In the years preceding the annual major league amateur draft, which was created in 1965 to even the playing field and provide teams with the worst record an opportunity to select the best talent, clubs tried to outbid each other. Scouting was of paramount importance. Baseball sleuths who failed to find great players or who misread a player's potential did not remain employed for long. Front office personnel such as general managers who consistently allowed rivals to snag eventual superstars without making a strong attempt to sign them were also routinely dispatched. Debates raged within organizations about the future of high school and college players.

There were few disagreements about me. I was universally wanted. Scouts viewed me as having a similar level of potential as Sandy Koufax, another left-hander who had in the late 1950s yet to blossom because despite averaging one strikeout per inning he could not consistently find the strike zone. I displayed excellent control in high school and other amateur competition. I consistently fanned at least two batters per inning because I not only threw a fastball that promised to get faster as I grew further into my body, but thanks greatly to my father I had developed major league–quality breaking pitches. It was no wonder that all sixteen major league teams made my parents an offer.

What was mind-boggling was my lack of appreciation for how their thirst for my services was about to affect my future. The perpetual fog I lived in that remained with me as I began my professional career included not recognizing where I was; not understanding my position; being desensitized to my environment; immaturity; depression; lack of a true sense of reality; and taking everything for granted. My career outlook was limited to having a little fun and getting paid for it.

The recruiting process began in earnest my sophomore year at Central Catholic when three scouts consistently attended my high school games in the spring and amateur league contests in the summer. They were not legally allowed to speak with me until graduation but they would periodically buy me ice cream after games. Among the scouts who showed a strong interest was Cy Williams with the Detroit Tigers. He lived in upstate New York but always drove down to watch me pitch. As a sophomore especially, but beyond as well, those visits had no effect on me. I did not recognize or understand the seriousness of his interest. He conversed often with my parents but not me. Williams sometimes drove me home from Colt League games when my coach (Jim Green) could not. He grew so close to my family that when I did not sign with the Tigers my sister refused to speak with me for a month.

My parents sheltered me from what became a bit of a circus as the number of scouts grew during my junior and senior years. Their protection played a role in my ignorance about what was happening to me but I do recall reading that the Pirates signed a California kid named Bob Bailey to the biggest bonus ever offered to an amateur player (Bailey never emerged as an All-Star but enjoyed a long and fruitful major league career) and I liked the idea. As a teenager who desperately sought attention, landing a huge bonus and receiving national media recognition for it was precisely what floated my boat.

My mother shunned that notion. She was not about to allow anyone else dictate the process of recruiting her seventeen-year-old son. The only club I thought about specifically through the whole thing was the Pirates and not because they were my hometown team but because of their $108,000 offer to Bailey. But my parents dictated everything. They insisted that there be no negotiations for my services. All major league teams were notified that they could pitch only one offer and that I and my parents would then make the final decision. I vividly recall sitting on the porch with Carol Ann and discussing the bids that had been placed.

Eventually the proposals were all in. My parents called me in to the dining room and handed me a list of teams and their offers. I noticed that eight of the sixteen presented bonuses of exactly $50,000, which led me to believe there was a bit of collusion involved. But when I feasted my eyes on the $75,000 deal offered by the Cleveland Indians, it was all over. That the Pirates gave Bob Bailey this same year a $108,000 bonus, I believe, was the main reason why they failed to offer any more than the stated $50,000 even though I was considered one of their favorites. What my parents apparently did not realize and I certainly did not since I never read the contract in its entirety was that part of that bonus was my salary for the next five years unless or until I reached the majors. I actually earned $160 per month for the next three months and nothing for winter instructional ball in St. Petersburg, Florida.

I knew little about Cleveland or the Indians, who had gained a reputation over the years for perennially strong pitching staffs. Among their premier talents had been another hard-throwing left-hander named Herb Score, who had appeared destined a few years earlier for a Hall of Fame career until a line drive by Yankees hitter Gil McDougald slammed into his eye. Score was never the same afterward. He had been traded to the White Sox by the time I made it to Cleveland in 1961. My first experience with Score came after I had been demoted to the Triple-A Jacksonville Suns in 1963. I had been assigned to stay in the same hotel as the visiting club. As luck would have it, one afternoon while I was eating before a night game, Score walked into the same dining room. He noticed that the waiter was talking baseball with me and asked if I was with the Suns. He invited me to eat with him, which I considered unreal because the opposition was considered the enemy in those days. He was always a very unpretentious and modest man, and I got to know him better in later years when he was a long-time broadcaster of Indians games on the radio.

It is somewhat unlucky that I signed with Cleveland after high school graduation in 1960. That was the first year of what became known to Indians fans as the Curse of Rocky Colavito. Three months before I signed and only a couple days before the regular season began, the hugely popular power-hitting outfielder had been traded to the Tigers for singles hitter Harvey Kuenn. The swap angered the vast majority of the fan base and even inspired protests in Cleveland. Though no one lousy trade can be responsible for decades of misery, the fact is the Indians remained at or near the bottom of the standings for the next thirty-three years. They did not vault back into contention until leaving Municipal

Stadium for Jacobs Field in 1994. Their massive struggle is one reason why, after competing in every playoff and World Series event in amateur baseball, I never came close to participating in a World Series in the professional ranks.

Not that I gave any thought to future Indians fortunes when I signed with the organization. I barely gave thought to my own future but I certainly received the kind of attention I always craved. I was invited to reveal my decision on the iconic, nationally televised game show *To Tell the Truth*, which aired on June 16, 1960. The experience numbed me but scared my mother, who was asked to travel with me since I was underage at only seventeen years old. She couldn't sleep the night before, which left her extremely tired. The network had a limousine deliver us to the hotel. We had separate rooms where we waited for our ride to the studio. When we got to what we were told was the green room—which was not green—my mom was escorted to the audience and I was told what to expect.

The program featured me as one of three contestants claiming to be Sam McDowell. A panel of stars that included actors Polly Bergen, Don Ameche, and Tom Poston hurled questions about baseball our way to determine before voting which one of us was the budding star. I towered over the other two contestants, though one of them certainly looked athletic enough to fool the guessers. The other was a bespectacled kid who looked nothing like a premier baseball prospect, and he gave himself away quickly by not knowing that Don Larsen threw the only perfect game in World Series history.

The questions were mostly a can of corn. I was asked, "What happens if a batter's bat tips the catcher's mitt?" I was a bit surprised at the obscurity of the question, which made me hesitate a bit before answering correctly that the hitter is awarded first base for interference. I was also asked the difference between a no-hitter and perfect game, who on the diamond rubs up a ball, and how a pitcher delivers a curve. I am not certain if my answers proved unsatisfactory to the panelists but only Poston guessed correctly. The other votes went to the other contestant who answered his baseball questions well enough to trick the other three.

I was a bit stiff during the show but I managed to crack a smile when I was told to stand up and reveal my identity as the audience clapped. My mother, meanwhile, sat proudly throughout. We later took in *The Sound of Music* on Broadway, for which a friend had procured us tickets. It was a dream come true for my mom but she was so tired she slept through the entire performance.

Soon I was off to Cleveland for a show-and-tell with the media. After watching a couple of my workouts, Indians pitching coach Mel Harder exclaimed, "All this kid needs is experience to pitch. He has all the mechanics and all the pitches." He was technically right. What he did not understand was that I was eons from being ready to adjust to better competition for there is far more to pitching than talent alone.

I returned home then left the next day for Lakeland, Florida, to launch my professional career. The Indians might have placed me higher in their organization than the Class D Lakeland Indians to start had my parents not insisted that I be sent to the lowest rung to get my feet wet. What the team did not know was that aside from the physical aspects of pitching, I was not prepared for any level. Coaches and managers back then never explored and dealt with the mental and emotional challenges faced by their players, let alone a seventeen-year-old kid leaving home for the first time. They worked on mechanics and considered the job done. Mechanics were not my problem. My father had made certain of that.

My numbness to the entire situation continued as I flew down to the Sunshine State. I felt nothing positive or negative about starting my career in Class D. I experienced no excitement, no dread, no nervousness. I was neither overconfident nor underconfident. I did not know what to expect partly because I gave it little consideration. The mechanical way I had gone through much of my life and athletic exploits continued. I could not even focus on the tasks at hand because they were part of this great unknown. Where was I going to stay? Who was going to greet me? Who was I going to meet? Where was I going to go when I got there? None of it even entered my mind until I arrived.

The answers to questions I never asked came soon enough. The Lakeland team trainer picked me up from the airport and delivered me to a house in which seven other players were staying. I later fetched my equipment bag and got a ride from my new teammates to the stadium, where I met manager Charlie Gassaway, who introduced me to the rest of the team. Upon dressing for my first game I realized I did not have the standard underwear. During my amateur playing days I simply put a jock strap over my underpants and then slid on my uniform. But these guys had special socks, special underpants, special undershirts, special socks. I purchased one and all from the clubhouse manager and finally looked like a professional ballplayer. From that point forward I watched my teammates carefully. Whatever they did, I did. It was a wise approach. I just wish I had not taken the same one a few years later when it came to drinking.

The $75,000 bonus provided by the Indians certainly put me in a higher tax bracket than my teammates, most of whom were at least a year or two older than me. But I did not spend it frivolously. I did purchase a Cadillac—I was so young I had to convince a teammate to sign for it—but only because the seven of us needed it as we were too cramped in just one car. And it was far from a bright, shiny new vehicle. It was a 1949 model with windows that did not work, which resulted in the frequent rains of Florida often splattering us as we drove along. It was no wonder the darn thing cost only $100. I learned late in the season that I had been assigned to winter ball in St. Petersburg after a month of vacation back in Pittsburgh so I simply parked the Cadillac by one of the many nearby Lakeland lakes and left it there. I came back a month later to find the car still there and in perfect working condition for my trip to St. Pete.

At one point while I was still in Lakeland my family drove down to watch me pitch. Our team was scheduled to play in a ballpark in Palatka built in what can best be described as a swamp. Rain would result in an overflow past the fence and bring in snakes, including water moccasins, and motivate outfielders to hightail it back to the bench. Sometimes we would notice spiders in our shoes when we finished games. Naturally we would want to clean ourselves after playing there but there were only three shower heads above a dirt floor.

I pitched the previous day; therefore I only had my running to do. So Gassaway allowed me to stay back as long as I got my exercise work done. But I learned that I had broken baseball etiquette. A player was not supposed to beg off unless he was on his deathbed. I learned that lesson again when Carol Ann was having our first baby. My manager and general manager then were adamant. I had to stay with the team. Fortunately times have changed.

Early in my professional career I received a rude awakening to the segregated South. I freaked out upon my arrival at the stadium in Lakeland when my eyes caught sight of a sign in front of the right-field seating that read "For Negroes Only." I was a northern kid who was ignorant of the racism of the Jim Crow period that had barely begun to erode. My father had worked with African Americans. I played alongside and against black people on every sports team in Pittsburgh. Great players were great players and bad players were bad players in my heart and mind. African Americans were in my classrooms and cafeterias in school. I never noticed differences based on race. But they were certainly treated differently on my team. When we took our few road trips we were forced to drop our black players off at a hotel where they would be accepted and we would go on to our hotel. I felt quite uneasy about it. I even witnessed my first cross burning in Lakeland but did not at that time know what it was. The whole experience was quite eerie.

I displayed a more humorous youthful ignorance of the ways of the world when we took our first road trip of the season to Daytona Beach. (Remember, I was only seventeen years old.) When we arrived at our Daytona Beach, I noticed many beautiful woman hanging out in the lobby. Later that day I asked a teammate if I would be permitted to date one of them after the game. He laughed his ass off but did not reveal why until we returned to the clubhouse to change into our uniforms. That is when he elicited the hearty laughter of my teammates by telling them of my intention. Why was everyone laughing at my expense? I eventually learned that those women were prostitutes. That they were in the hotel lobby came as no surprise to the older guys, including the veterans of minor league baseball who were accustomed to staying in cheap hotels also frequented by ladies of the night. I had learned my lesson by the time I advanced to Triple-A when we stumbled upon another house of ill-repute. It was the Peachtree Manor in Atlanta, where we played before the Braves moved there from Milwaukee. And no, I never "dated" any of them.

It is hard to believe that my baseball career had not risen to the top of my priority list at that time. I was still a kid playing a man's game. My focus and attention on my pitching would affect everything in my personal and professional life. But I did not grasp the concept. I did not understand the importance of how well I performed. I never looked forward to my future. Rather, I took everything day to day, moment to moment. I anticipated the end of my first professional season so I could enjoy mindless pursuits such as simply hanging out with Carol.

I was not destined to spend much time with her. Two weeks after I got back to Pittsburgh I received a plane ticket to St. Petersburg for winter ball. Soon I was back in the same environment, which exacerbated my existing emotional and mental problems. I felt like I did not belong. I suspected irrationally that I had not earned my way to that level. I believed that my teammates, many of whom boasted two or three or four years of experience, were superior to me. I placed them on a pedestal, viewed them as icons. I vividly recall my first day of winter ball heading into the training room for a Band-Aid after cutting myself and seeing teammate Bob Gordon conversing with another player from the training table. Just saying hello to them I felt like I was interfering. I felt so uncomfortable about that encounter that I did not interact with Bob the rest of the season.

The mindset that I was not worthy of attention or had not earned my status in the game made me feel awkward with all the publicity I received in Pittsburgh immediately after signing the huge bonus with the Indians and beyond. I was asked to speak at various functions, including my old high school, which made me feel uncomfortable. I was uneasy because in my mind I had not accomplished anything yet. Never mind that I had earned that bonus as the most accomplished prep pitcher in America. I did not see myself that way.

I have written about my existence as a kid in the fog of an alcoholic personality. I have written about my narcissism and craving for attention. And perhaps at that point in my life only the desire to be accepted inspired me to want to help others in need. Or maybe a positive aspect of my personality that would be allowed to realize itself in counseling well after I retired from baseball was emerging.

One example revolved around my mother. I had sat down with her after returning from Lakeland following my first pro ball experience. I asked her for an update, and she complained about the cost of the home mortgage. Rather than offer to help, I could only think about spending time with my girlfriend. But when I got back to Pittsburgh following winter ball I took more of an interest in the financial concerns of my mom. I asked her the balance on the mortgage and she blurted out $10,000. So I wrote a check for that amount and handed it to her. She shed tears of happiness. At first she refused to accept the money but she did eventually, and it felt wonderful to relieve some of her worries and stress. It was a rare spark of selflessness from self-centered Sam.

But it was not the only one. In spring training the following year I played a role in the rescue of an endangered woman and it made me feel good. The rather harrowing story began in Tucson, where I was working out with the Indians before my transfer to minor league camp in Daytona Beach. I befriended an attractive waitress while staying at the Roadway Inn—nothing flirtatious about our relationship or with any intention. One day another waitress sidled up next to me and asked if I knew her colleague and I confirmed that I did. She told me that her friend's divorced husband had pretty much kidnapped her and her son in the middle of the night and taken them to his house in the middle of the desert. I learned that the waitress I had been talking to was afraid to inform the police. So I did.

We drove with the policeman to the residence and he rescued the woman and her child. But she had no place to go. She had been living with the waitress who informed me of the kidnapping and her three children and had been looking for a permanent home. So she thankfully and gratefully accepted my offer to put her up in a hotel. I paid for her stay until she could find a place of her own. Soon the husband called the Indians and even my mother complaining about my involvement and making up lies about the incident. He claimed I was still interfering, which was a fantasy since I had already left for Daytona Beach.

That is where we stayed in an old army barracks and practiced every day on a field filled with fire ants that enjoyed biting us. But I was content just to be playing ball and getting paid for it. I rarely thought about anything in particular. That complacency prevented me from understanding anything that was happening to me in my personal and professional life. I spent time walking up and down the boardwalk with teammates, winning stuffed animals by shooting little basketballs into little rims, and then being asked by shady carnies not to come back because I was simply too accurate.

I often recall more vividly than anything that happened in games the camaraderie and funny moments outside the realm of competition during my early playing days. That is certainly true of my first winter ball experience. I remember watching with my teammates the 1960 World Series between the Pirates and Yankees. Though I still knew little about major league baseball, I had become aware of a few of the Pittsburgh players while pitching batting practice at Forbes Field, and I joined in the celebration around the tube when Bill Mazeroski slugged the only series-clinching home run in the history of that fall classic. He mashed it off Yankees pitcher Ralph Terry, who it turns out spent time as my roommate with the Indians in 1965.

Those who have complained with some justification that my poor control prevented me from maximizing my potential must learn the story of Steve Dalkowski. The Baltimore organization pitcher became the talk of the Grapefruit League in the early 1960s. The buzz became so great that I could hardly wait for our scheduled game against a group of Orioles minor leaguers. Dalkowski is believed to this day to have been the hardest thrower in the history of the sport, yet his inability to fire strikes would forever keep him out of the major leagues. His reputation seemed well-earned to me after watching him pitch and hearing the sound of his fastball cracking into the catcher's mitt. That great stuff does not make one a superior pitcher becomes obvious if you track the career of Dalkowski. I was learning that lesson myself at the same time.

I realized during my first year in professional ball and then later what I should have known before my career began. The talent differential between the amateur game in Pittsburgh and even the lowest rung of the minor leagues was vast. Plus there were so many intricacies about pitching that I needed to learn. It was mind-boggling. But rather than soak in as much knowledge as possible, I continued to live in a fantasy world. I remained in a fog, interested only in having fun and getting paid for it even after the Indians catapulted me from Class D to the Triple-A Salt Lake City Bees to start the 1961 season.

I tried in vain to pitch as I did in the amateur ranks and get away with it. Harder was correct when he told the assembled media in Cleveland that I boasted the perfect mechanics and an assortment of pitches to thrive at the major league level once I got a bit of seasoning. But what neither he nor I understood was that I had never been forced to learn the nuances of my craft and the strategies required to maximize my vast talents. In high school I simply fired fastballs by the average hitters and mixed in a few sharp-breaking curves against the better ones. The results were overwhelming. But there were no average hitters in professional ball, not even in Class D. They were the cream of the crop from the high school and college programs. I had very good control against amateur competition. My condition and daily throwing program had made my body, shoulders, and arms strong. By the time I got to Lakeland I was throwing harder than ever. But I struggled greatly with my control.

I did not comprehend this, nor did I learn why it was happening for several years. What I noticed was that I could no longer throw my fastball by hitters even though I had attained greater speed on it. My velocity did not scare hitters as it did in high school. I also could not get away with mistakes anymore. When I hung a curveball, it got hit hard rather than fouled off. I compared my situation to the amateur all-star games I pitched in when I faced the best hitters in the city. About three or four hitters in the lineup provided a challenge yet I was still throwing no-hitters and one-hitters. But in the minors everyone I faced was an all-star from his city. And they had all progressed from their prep days. I had to improve as well but that did not happen until I shed my robotic approach, until frustration and anger forced me to learn the strategies of pitching. That watershed moment was not exactly right around the bend.

I had previously not needed to throw quality strikes. My pure stuff overwhelmed batters. In professional ball I would not survive unless I hit the corners, moved the ball to all four quadrants, mixed up my pitches. I pitched more fearfully than confidently. The result was my first experience with control issues that would haunt me throughout my career, though I learned to overcome them during my best seasons. I walked 80 batters in just 104 innings during my one year at Lakeland but still won about half my decisions and compiled a respectable 3.35 ERA by escaping jams on pure stuff. I learned quickly that pro ball would be no walk in the park unless I cut down on all those walks in the park.

The problem was neither physical nor mental. It was immaturity. I required an adjustment. I needed to gain an awareness of the science of pitching. My teammates understood. They respected that I was trying as hard as I could. They knew I had received a huge bonus, but there was no resentment that I could detect. The control problems stemmed from watching the same stuff that baffled amateur hitters getting slammed for line drives. But that was the only stuff I had.

I had to become a pitcher, not a thrower. It would not happen overnight but the Indians were not about to wait. Rather than move me along slowly through the system to accommodate the wishes of my parents, they had skyrocketed me to the Triple-A Salt Lake City Bees in 1961, my first full season in professional ball. I spoke years later with co–minor league director Bob Kennedy about what some would perceive as an undeserved major promotion, and he told me the organization had wanted to challenge me to see if I could handle it.

I could not handle it—at least in regard to control. I managed to compile a 13-10 record as the only starter on the club with a winning record. I kept my team in most games. But nobody was teaching me how to pitch. Batters remained quite satisfied taking my offerings and jogging to first base. My wildness became more pronounced. I walked 152 batters in 175 innings as my ERA ballooned more than a point from a respectable 3.35 with Lakeland to a loftier 4.42.

At least I stayed sober despite a curiosity about drinking that nearly sent Salt Lake City manager Freddie Fitzsimmons into spontaneous combustion. Fitzsimmons was a standout pitcher for the New York Giants in the 1920s and 1930s and managed a terrible Phillies club during World War II. He was sixty years old when he was managing me with the Bees. One vow I made upon the start of my professional career in my ever-present desire to draw attention to myself was to stay away from booze. After all, most players drank a beer or two after games. They were even supplied by the teams in the clubhouse. That remained my motivation until I discovered that I could draw more attention drunk and that boozing temporarily strengthened my confidence in social situations and made me feel more normal. Anyway, one very hot day I gave in to temptation and had started to drink a beer when Fitzsimmons bolted from his office screaming about the mental mistakes we had made in the game. He then noticed me drinking the beer and embarked on another rant. "What the hell are you doing?" he yelled. Message delivered. I did not take another sip the rest of the year.

Teetotaler Sam walked nearly twice as many batters as any Salt Lake City pitcher that year but he posted its only winning record—we were quite a poor club. And the Indians were eager to show off their flame-throwing bonus baby. My major league debut was right around the corner.

5

THE DEBUT

The Indians brought me up for a show-off start against the Twins on September 15, 1961. I do not recall if I knew that the Twins boasted the premier offensive club in baseball, but facing the likes of Harmon Killebrew, Earl Battey, and Bobby Allison certainly presented a challenge for a kid still six days from his nineteenth birthday.

Though it was a cold night, that only 4,500 patrons clicked through the turnstiles at Cleveland Municipal Stadium for my major league debut shows how turned off Indians fans had become since the trade of Rocky Colavito to Detroit.

Like most ballplayers, I recall vividly everything about my first taste of the big leagues. I was surprised to have been promoted though I did sport the only winning record among the Salt Lake City starters despite a rather high ERA. My teammates and I spent much time discussing who would and would not get the call. I never considered myself a hotshot—that lack of confidence was part of my problem—so I figured I fell into the latter category.

I drove all the way from Salt Lake City to Cleveland in a white Thunderbird along with teammates Max Alvis and Jim Lawrence (who received two at-bats at the end of the season and never returned to the big leagues). I had purchased the car with my bonus money after my first experience in winter instructional league. The three of us were jam-packed against all our suitcases and equipment bags but did not stop until we arrived, instead taking turns driving and sleeping.

I was not only younger and more immature than Alvis and Lawrence but my lack of interest in major league baseball when I was growing up resulted in a lack of knowledge about the guys I was about to play with. I knew little about the Indians except some of their names like Woodie Held, Gary Bell, Chuck

Essegian, Tito Francona, and Vic Power—and of course Jimmy Piersall, my roomie during spring training. The entire experience was like a journey into the unknown. I was in awe walking into the Cleveland clubhouse for the first time—seeing how big it was in comparison to our facilities in Salt Lake City though miniscule by today's standards.

I was nervous, which looking back was a positive emotion because at least I was feeling *something*. I had to that point gone through life on and off the field robotically. Essegian took the lead in a very kind, caring way in trying to put me at ease. I appreciate that to this day because back in that era new teammates rarely befriended rookies until they had earned their way onto a major league roster. One example was Bell taking me out two years later for what became my first drinking binge after he'd concluded I deserved the attention of a baseball veteran.

The calming presence of Essegian proved to have a positive effect. With my parents, sister, and brother-in-law in the stands—they all drove over from Pittsburgh—I outpitched Twins starter and future Cleveland teammate Jack Kralick into the seventh inning though, typically, I walked five. I would have earned the victory had reliever Frank Funk not blown the save after maintaining a 2-0 lead with two outs in the ninth. I might have hurled a complete-game shutout had I not broken two ribs trying to throw too hard in chilly temperatures.

It has been sixty years but I still remember the pitch that sent me out of the game. It was a 2-2 fastball I fired to Clevelander and future Indians teammate Rich Rollins in my eagerness to strike him out. It resulted in ball three and the broken ribs. I was dispatched to the hospital for x-rays that determined I was done for the year. No biggie—the season was almost over and after the examination my parents accompanied me to a wonderful ice cream parlor on Euclid Avenue that specialized in fancy sundaes. I was healed in time for winter ball in Puerto Rico.

That first full season in professional baseball tested me both socially and professionally. I had been forced away from family and friends in my comfortable, familiar little Pittsburgh bubble and thrown unprepared mentally or emotionally into an entirely new world. I was not alone. Other rookies to the pro game were trying to handle the same experience. But my self-centered and alcoholic personality driven by narcissism prevented me from realizing that we were all in the same boat. I only cared about how my new life was affecting me.

I recall vividly my first spring training in Tucson in 1961. Upon my arrival in Arizona I checked into my hotel room, unpacked my bags, hung up my clothes, and flipped on the television set. I began reading the printed material provided by the Indians about the ins and outs of camp when my designated roommate entered. It was none other than Piersall, whose emotional issues on and off the field would eventually inspire the movie *Fear Strikes Out*. He stepped about ten feet into the room and stared at me. "Hi, I'm Sam McDowell," I said with a friendly tone. "I'm not rooming with a rookie," he replied in a rather unfriendly tone before grabbing his two suitcases and marching out. Piersall was not about to share a room with a first-year player. So I stayed by myself for three weeks until leaving for Daytona. Single rooms, especially for rookies, in spring training or the regular season were unheard of in those days.

That my personality allowed me to remain unaffected by events that for other teenagers might have proven traumatic was not necessarily a bad thing. But I was overwhelmed by the company I kept. Even though the vast majority of players in camp were ordinary minor leaguers or mildly accomplished major leaguers, I saw them all in my eighteen-year-old mind as superstars. I sat in the clubhouse looking around in awe. That feeling was more memorable to me than any of the rather uneventful happenings on the field.

I experienced what I feared to be my first bit of trouble as a professional player during that short spring training stint in Tucson, though it was not my fault. We were in Mesa playing against the Cubs. Indians manager Jimmy Dykes, as is customary for exhibitions, had scheduled his pitchers for that game and I was not among them. Around the seventh inning Harder asked me and several others to clear the bench, take a shower, and leave the facility so there would be enough room for everyone in what was the tiniest clubhouse in the Cactus League. But when Gary Bell hurt his ankle, Dykes ordered Harder to call me in to pitch. He should have been able to find me in the shower—that is where I had been ordered to go. Never mind logic. Dykes called me over on the bus returning to Tucson and informed me that I had been fined. I complained that I had been told to take a shower and he replied that I should have been ready anyway. It turned out the joke was on me, just a typical gag played on a rookie. There was a fine of five cigars.

I took it in stride. No green kid was going to rebel against his manager. I yearned to stay on his good side but I also wanted to show that two could play that game. The next morning I visited the glass case in the hotel lobby and picked out the four cheapest, lousiest cigars I could find as a way to "pay my fine" to Dykes. They cost me a total of twenty cents. I presented them to my cigar-loving manager who told me in no uncertain terms that those "ropes" did not befit a man of his stature. I returned to the glass case and purchased the most expensive cigars I could find—set me back four bucks—and handed them to Dykes. All was well.

My fine performance against the Twins proved a bit of an anomaly for that point in my career. I actually regressed statistically over the next couple years as

I bounced from the big leagues to the minors and received no help from anyone in trying to transform from a thrower to a pitcher. My struggles on the mound became more pronounced. And worsening issues off the field did not just nearly cost me my career. They almost cost me my life.

My arm was that of a man among boys. My head and heart were those of a boy among men. My immaturity was battling my talent in the early 1960s. And my talent was losing. The loneliness, sadness, and depression that plagued me as a child only worsened in my early years as a professional athlete. I remained in a fog with neither the motivation nor direction necessary to stick and thrive in the Show.

No conscious thoughts about my craft entered my brain as I stood on the mound, executed my windup, and delivered. Ignorance was not bliss. I felt I had to be satisfied getting paid for playing a game because I had no idea how to maximize my effectiveness. I boasted far more ability than my peers yet I was in awe of them. I was twenty going on twelve.

Mechanics were not the problem. My father used his expertise in engineering and anatomy to explain to a young Sam McDowell the inner workings of the human body and how it can be best contorted to execute the most effective windup, arm angle, release point, and delivery. But my ignorance of the science of pitching prevented me from taking that knowledge and running with it. I also lacked focus and concentration. I understood nothing of the strategy of pitching. How could I get hitters out consistently and efficiently? I couldn't.

It proves that scouting is an inexact science. Harder was only partly right when he claimed after my three-day workout in Cleveland at age seventeen that all I required was experience. He was correct that I boasted the capacity to unleash a wicked variety of pitches. My stuff often trumped my ignorance of the science of pitching. I could sometimes overwhelm hitters with my velocity and movement. But I could not reliably throw strikes. And I certainly could not locate within the strike zone. Heck, I was giving nearly one batter per inning a red carpet to first base. They understood that my wildness motivated me to fire multiple fastballs in a row. No pitcher throws hard enough to blow away professional hitters with heater after heater. They were eventually going to time it up and destroy mine, especially when I could not spot them. Learning and embracing the science and strategy of my craft would have allowed me to overcome my poor control and maximize the effectiveness of each pitch in my repertoire. But I was throwing in a fog through which I could not see. Little did I understand at the time that the fog was part of a disease about which I remained unaware.

I simply tried to outguess opposing hitters in what often resulted in a losing struggle. The coaches were no help. Rather than teaching me what to throw to particular hitters on particular counts and *why*, they grew frustrated with me. Among them was Indians manager Birdie Tebbetts, who after taking over the job in 1963 decided to call all my pitches from the dugout. At no time did he sit me down and explain his reasoning so I was forced to take the initiative. I asked him twice why he was dictating my pitch selection and he replied unsatisfactorily on both occasions that I should just follow along and he would transform me into—his words—a superstar. It was not the first time he uttered that proclamation. He told me the same thing when I arrived for spring training.

Wrong. He only prevented me from growing as a person and as a pitcher. I did not need any help in that department—we were working in tandem on maintaining my lack of maturity. I had no idea what I was doing on the mound. I was simply trying to throw fastballs by hitters or bouncing curveballs in the dirt in the hope they would swing.

I can understand in retrospect the immediate motivation for Tebbetts to call my pitches. He was trying to win ballgames. The job security of any major league manager is precarious. But his efforts backfired. I lacked the emotional investment game to game, knowing that I was not fully responsible for my performance. I pitched no better in 1963 than I had in 1962 when I bounced from Salt Lake City to Cleveland. I performed far better in the minors than I did with the Indians. I allowed 144 hits and 114 walks in 152 innings during those two seasons combined. Yielding one hit per inning is fine for most pitchers but it was inexcusable for one with my talent.

I was only twenty years old chronologically with the maturity level of a young teenager. The goal should have been development. Rather than groom me into a pitcher who could thrive by teaching me the game within the game then allowing me to execute what I had learned, the Indians were stifling me. I had an excuse for my failures. I could blame them on somebody else. Nobody—not Sandy Koufax, not Nolan Ryan, not Aroldis Chapman—boasts the velocity to fire nothing but fastballs for strikes and thrive against major league hitters. That certainly applied to Sam McDowell, who by that time could match miles per hour with the best of them. Though radar readings were a futuristic concept in the early 1960s, it can surely be ascertained that I was throwing at over 100 miles per hour given that I was clocked at 103 well past my prime in the mid-1970s and was determined to have boasted the third-fastest fastball in major league history.

Like Koufax and Ryan, I struggled mightily with control early in my professional career. Such was not a problem in amateur ball. High school batters could not catch up to my fastball and flailed away at curves that featured far more break than anything they had previously seen. But as I grew physically after signing with the Indians, my fastball gained even more speed. It was no wonder that *Cleveland Plain Dealer* writer Bob Dolgan nicknamed me "Sudden Sam" when I first arrived in major league camp in March 1961 and the established slugger Harmon Killebrew exclaimed that my fastball arrived "all of a sudden." The problem was the faster I could throw, the faster I wanted to throw. By the end of the 1961 season I was overthrowing it.

That exacerbated my existing control problem, which was based on weak confidence and concentration. My wildness was not only a reflection of fear of getting hit. It was also a combination of poor focus brought about by lack of faith in my knowledge and abilities as well as myself in general. It did not help when right fielder Bob Nieman misjudged an easy fly ball that fell for a hit then came back to the dugout and before anyone could say anything, spouted, "I shouldn't be out there as a caddy for a rookie pitching."

In order for a pitcher to master control and location, he must believe if he throws a pitch toward a certain spot, the odds are a positive result will prevail. At that time I doubted I could ever throw a pitch to a certain spot. I hoped for an area. I had neither trust nor the courage to gamble on the outcome. It became a chicken-and-egg problem. I did not have the focus to feel confident on the mound. And I did not feel confident enough in my focus to throw confidently.

The numbers proved it. From my professional debut in 1961 to the end of June 1963, after the experiment of calling pitches by Tebbetts had failed and the Indians returned me to Triple-A Jacksonville, I had walked 374 batters in 478 2/3 innings combined in the minors and majors. Issuing seven walks per nine innings, especially given that such wildness precludes locating within the strike zone, is a recipe for disaster. Making matters worse was that my hits-to-innings-pitched ratio was rising. It is no wonder that my ERA during my first two full seasons in Cleveland soared to an ugly 5.79. Yeah, I was barely out of my teenage years. But I was too darn talented to post such horrible numbers.

The failure I experienced from the start of my major league career threatened to become ingrained in me. The realities for young hurlers in that era, decisions made by the Indians, and my own crisis of confidence conspired to hold me back starting in 1962 after I had made the team out of spring training.

All pitchers at that time were forced to overcome the uncertainty of whether they would be used as a starter or reliever in the big leagues. Few were groomed as either. The better pitchers generally started and the leftovers were used out of the bullpen despite exceptions such as Dick Radatz. The modern era in which relievers with explosive stuff are trained as setup men and closers was decades away. I wonder if I would have eventually been projected as a closer given my over 100 mph fastball and sharp-breaking slider and curve. But the great unknown of whether I would start or relieve, often on a day's notice, did not help me prepare for my next outing.

Compounding the problem in 1962 was Mel McGaha, the former major league pitcher who preceded Tebbetts as Indians manager and resident pitch-caller for Sam McDowell. McGaha bounced me from the bullpen into the rotation like a Super Ball. He dictated my selection when I pitched in relief, setting up a special signal from the dugout to catcher John Romano. Perhaps McGaha felt justified in his actions when I allowed 15 earned runs and 18 walks in just 11 2/3 innings over 4 starts and just 3 runs in 13 2/3 innings and 3 walks in 7 performances out of the bullpen. But he was doing me no favors. The goal was to transform me into a pitcher whose outcomes matched his abilities. As McGaha, Tebbetts, and future Indians manager Joe Adcock failed to learn in future years, calling my pitches did not place me on the road to realizing my potential. It only exacerbated all the internal problems I was having.

Meanwhile, my body and life were changing. During much of high school I was a six-footer carrying 180 pounds. Then I continued to grow only in one direction. I eventually shot up five-and-a-half inches yet did not gain a pound. The Indians grew alarmed as I went from solid to skinny. They sent me to the Mayo Clinic and Cleveland Clinic to launch a weight-gain plan that included downing milkshakes, vitamins, and protein mixes. I gained nary a pound. Then I married Carol Ann in the winter of 1962. By 1963 I had started to gain weight. She fattened me up with three squares a day, and when I arrived at spring training I tipped the scales at 220. Birdie immediately demanded I lose the weight I had gained. I did that, but I slowly added a few pounds over the next few years and spent most of my career at about 220.

The most dramatic change would occur a year later. Call it an awakening, call it an epiphany. I had not before 1964 felt an insatiable drive to succeed. I was a merely a child playing a game. I was in fantasy land. I had little idea what I was doing and had no map to find my way. But a sense of pride and intense anger erupted within me that spring. The seeds of my discontent were planted when Tebbetts again began calling my pitches and I allowed a home run into a strong wind to Giants slugger Orlando Cepeda that to this day remains in orbit. I received after the game a message from Birdie that he and general manager Gabe Paul wanted to meet with me back at the hotel. That is when I was told of yet another demotion, this time to Portland, where the organization had moved its Triple-A affiliate.

I was incensed. I was hurt. In retrospect I realize that after my poor performance in spring training the move was justified, but I also understand that nobody had been willing or had the foresight to help me grow as a pitcher. My rage inspired me to inform Paul that I would refuse to return to Cleveland if Tebbetts was still calling my pitches. His reply was equally forceful. He threatened to "bury me in the minor leagues."

I can still feel the anger I experienced leaving the hotel room, packing my stuff for minor league camp, and moving it all to the another complex and motel. A psychologist sitting with me could write a five-thousand-page paper on the changes that were taking place within me mentally and emotionally at that time.

Former Yankees pitcher Jim Bouton once wrote in his controversial 1970 book *Ball Four* that the minor leagues were all very minor after he had been demoted. He was right. Once you experience the majors you always feel cheapened being sent down. It is one thing for kids rising through the system who know they are still being seasoned to accept a stint in the minors. It is quite another for someone like me who had pitched in the big leagues in each of the past three seasons to get banished again, especially given my anger at what I rightfully perceived as a lack of teaching from the coaching staff.

The minor leagues indeed felt all very minor. The locker rooms were much smaller and dank. The competition was weaker—I had finally gained enough understanding to feel that it was beneath my talents. And the daily allowance was certainly smaller. My teammates in Portland, who knew that I was earning a higher salary, frequently asked to borrow money so I set up a system in which I charged 20 percent interest if they did not pay me back within a week. I figured justifiably that minor leaguers could not afford that, and so they returned what they borrowed on time. But I was not a bank. I was a pitcher whose career was at a crossroads. My back was against the proverbial wall. I was furious.

The event proved cathartic. For the first time I felt motivated by a sense of pride and purpose. I had experienced an awakening.

6

BETTER PITCHER, BIGGER BOOZER

During the first four years of my career I listened to everybody and anybody who had a theory on pitching and tried to do everything they told me, which was impossible and confusing. From that point forward I was determined to learn on my own by asking questions and studying. I talked to catchers and hitters I respected. I gained knowledge by watching how pitchers set up and retired certain batters by changing speeds and location. I noted batting stances and how pitchers exploited weaknesses. I discussed the science of hitting and pitching. I examined release points and how they affected break. I analyzed which pitches hitters swung at and which they laid off. I studied where they stood in the box and if they moved based on various counts.

Prime example: When I watched Mickey Mantle during batting practice I noticed, despite the great hitter he was, he had a little circular space inside and just above his hands that he would loop under the pitch with his bat. Once I started pitching him there with my fastball I had a little advantage. But if I got it out away from him or even down, forget it. I was doomed. This was different from our scouting report. Each team has a specialist who charts opposing hitters and maintains a record of pitchers faced. They also notice different speeds from opposing hitters and what the reaction was. The chart would show what the hitter did with a curveball, a changeup, or a slider. With the reports and my stuff I could get away with many areas and types of pitches others could not. Thus my strikeouts of the Mick.

I could not take advantage of everything I discovered immediately, but most importantly I was taking personal responsibility for my craft and career for the first time. Portland skipper Johnny Lipon, who later managed me in Cleveland, vowed to let me figure out my own pitch selection. I could have hugged him for that. His approach was like a breath of fresh air. He sat me down the first day and told me that he was simply going to leave me alone and allow me to take the mound every fourth day.

He indeed left me to my devices, unlike Tebbetts and the major league coaches who told me when to sneeze and cough. They had ingrained in me the notion that my stuff was so good that I could thrive throwing the ball anywhere over the plate. That is not pitching. Lipon gave me confidence by insisting that I had no control problem. He would discuss the art of pitching with me after games and suggest what I had done wrong from the viewpoint of a hitter. But he never called a pitch.

I did have a control problem psychologically before 1964. But I began learning to control my emotions, which allowed me to gain control on the mound both literally and figuratively. The results were phenomenal. I embarked on one of the greatest runs in the history of minor league baseball. My newfound knowledge bred confidence, which I learned through the study of psychology can only be achieved by accomplishing something planned and worthwhile. My anger bred determination. My talent bred dominance. I won all eight decisions with Portland and compiled a ridiculous 1.18 ERA. I struck out 102 batters in 76 innings. I threw three consecutive shutouts, including a no-hitter. And most shocking was that I walked just twenty-four—amazing indeed considering my seven-walks-per-nine-innings ratio over my first three professional seasons.

That success empowered me. After I had won my seventh straight start I received a call from Indians general manager Gabe Paul, who congratulated me and told me to hop on a plane to Los Angeles the next morning because I was to start against the Angels. I am certain he expected me to jump for joy. But instead I asked him if Tebbetts was going to continue calling my pitches when he returned (he had suffered a heart attack in early April and would not be back until July). Paul gave me the same "Don't act like that" line he uttered when I was demoted so I told him to forget bringing me back until my freedom on the mound was guaranteed. Paul threatened again to bury me in the minors and hung up the phone.

I was not trying to be vengeful. I had learned from experience that I could succeed on my own rather than perform like a robot under the control of my manager. I was not pretending to be a know-it-all. Rather, I found some of the secrets to success and did not want to lose them all by battling Birdie. Soon I was on a plane to Hawaii for another start and another dominant victory.

That latest notch in my belt was only one ace up my sleeve. I was keenly aware that Paul could not keep me in the minors all season because under major league rules he would then make me eligible for a draft in which any team could pick me up for nothing. And considering I was still just twenty-one and finally blossoming, the chances of the Indians letting me leave were nil. Paul called again and promised that Tebbetts would no longer call my pitches. That was all I needed to hear. I was on the next flight to the nation's capital, where the team was facing the Senators. My career was about to take off.

I arrived back in the Show white-hot and stayed that way. I beat Washington in relief, striking out six in just three-and-a-third innings, then joined the rotation. All was not perfect—my walk ratio increased as major league hitters proved more adept at laying off pitches out of the zone, and I still did not feel confident enough to challenge the best with fastballs. But the determination to succeed and the lessons learned with Portland allowed me to remain on a roll. I struck out fourteen in a complete-game victory over the White Sox in my first start back, then followed it up with a defeat of the Senators and a shutout against Kansas City. I did not win again for nearly two months but that was far more a reflection of meager run support than my effectiveness. I pitched well in 11 of the first 12 outings after my promotion, at which point I owned a 2.68 ERA and 87 strikeouts in 77 innings.

Then Birdie began to chirp again. One poor effort in Yankee Stadium against the perennial American League champions set him off. He decided in the third inning to send pitch signals to catcher Johnny Romano from the dugout. I was infuriated—again. He removed me from the game in the sixth inning then continued to call my pitches during a terrible start against Baltimore. His interference was messing with my head on the mound and negatively affecting my performance. It was a game sadly in which I had some of my best stuff ever and it was all thrown away by Tebbetts's interference.

He was again stifling my growth. That stuck in my craw well into the 1966 season. After a start against the Orioles that year I marched to the clubhouse to complain about Tebbetts. Reporter Russell Schneider asked me later if I had demanded his ouster and I denied it. But by that time the choice was clear. Tebbetts was eventually fired, and I was told that my ultimatum played a critical role.

The difference in the Sam McDowell of 1964 was that I had matured enough to channel my anger into positive energy. I rebounded to pitch well in August and finished with a sizzling September in which I won all six decisions, including two against the Yankees during which I allowed no earned runs.

I could have taken that momentum and launched myself into a Hall of Fame career. I boasted as much pure talent as any pitcher of my generation. I had just turned twenty-two. Yeah, I still lacked control. But so did another left-hander by the name of Sandy Koufax when he was that age. Koufax did not find his groove until he was twenty-five. And walks did not preclude Nolan Ryan from skyrocketing to superstardom. He led the league eight times in that dubious department and allowed more free passes than any pitcher in baseball history, yet his bust sits proudly in Cooperstown. Ryan had the stuff to overcome base runners. So did I—and I had better control. Granted, poor run support would prevent me from maximizing my win total. But my vow to take personal responsibility for my career precluded making excuses.

Only I could stop Sam McDowell. And I did. I had already planted the seeds of personal destruction.

It was 1963. We were in Chicago and I accompanied friend and teammate Gary Bell along with Barry Latman to the Jim Diamond Steakhouse for dinner. We were celebrating a victory. Baseball players in my era and beyond embraced a drinking culture. But I had never traveled down that road until that night. Bell ordered a drink, so I ordered the same drink. He downed another one, so did I. Every time Bell called for more I did the same. I did not like the taste. It burned my throat. But Bell was a popular player, and I embraced the notion of being one of the boys. So after he left and went back to the hotel to rest, I continued down Michigan Avenue and visited all the bars on the way back to the hotel.

I enjoyed the effects of alcohol. The buzz made my happy and peaceful. The loneliness and depression that had permeated my very being since childhood dissipated. I had succeeded in my desire to feel like a normal person. I knew nothing about the chemical changes that occurred in me when alcohol reached the stomach and intestines and flowed directly into the blood system. That was an eye-opening education I received two decades later. When I drank I went from a continuing malaise to instantly feeling giddy, happy, accepted. I felt like one of the crowd. What I perceived as positive effects, of course, were merely temporary. But that only served to strengthen my desire to drink. My obsessive-compulsive personality eventually resulted in a struggle to moderate when I did partake.

The impact on my life and career was immeasurable. I did not believe at the time it adversely influenced my pitching—my 1964 epiphany was right around the corner, I would a year later embark on arguably my finest season, and I had emerged with a plan that I believed would stop drunkenness from affecting my mental state on the mound. Little did I understand at any point before I drank myself out of baseball how devastating alcoholism was to my livelihood. My roller-coaster career of dizzying heights and dismal lows had scarcely begun.

My marriage and my very life were soon to be endangered. The temporary departure of Carol motivated my suicide attempt. One can only imagine the ramifications if the Indians and the general public had learned that I had tried to take my life. The trauma of being demoted to Portland a few months later cannot compare to that of an attempted suicide but it was certainly easier to change the approach to my career than to alter my entire lifestyle, no matter how harmful. I felt occasional drunkenness would not weaken my performances on the mound as long as I was sober as I prepared for my next start and while I was pitching. There is some logic to that. Heck, Pirates pitcher Dock Ellis claimed he threw a no-hitter in 1970 while tripping on LSD (though I have my doubts, even though he reaffirmed it years later as a teammate with the Pirates, because he craved attention even more than I did). All I was doing was getting drunk on occasion several days before I took the mound.

There were exceptions but even those cemented the contention I made in my own mind that I could mix some boozing in with my career. One night while pitching for Portland in 1964 I accompanied power-hitting catcher Duke Sims (who has remained a close friend years after catching me with the Indians) on a late-night drinking binge that had me back at the hotel around 3:30 am. Not much time for sleep—I had to get up four hours later for an 11 a.m. game. As I was eating breakfast I noticed Lipon coming down the steps so I placed a newspaper in front of my face so he could not tell I had been out almost all night. The upshot is that I threw a no-hitter that day. Then I returned to the hotel, plopped into bed, and stayed there until the next morning. I slept twelve straight hours.

I never returned to the minor leagues after my breakthrough in 1964. But I also never returned to the minor leagues of drinking. By that time I had begun boozing more frequently. I had started down the path followed by all alcoholics and it would continue throughout my career, increasing the number of times I would drink and the regularity of my drunkenness. From 1964 to 1967 I drank about twice a month. I had yet to become an angry drunkard, a man who engaged in fistfights in bars and had to be bailed out of jail by his wife or employer.

Though I did not yet recognize my alcoholic personality, I was not drinking often enough or untimely enough to adversely influence my pitching physically. In fact, though I compiled a wonderful 1.81 ERA in 1968 and managed my only 20-win season in 1970, it can be argued that 1965 was my finest year. I recorded the best ERA in the American League at 2.18 and struck out 325 batters, the most in the league since Indians legend Bob Feller fanned 348 in 1946 and the second-highest total since 1904. The difference is that Feller compiled his total in 371 innings. I did it in 273, which means from a pure statistical standpoint I would have struck out 441 had I remained on the mound as long as Bullet Bob did that year. Only two American League pitchers (Nolan Ryan and Gerrit Cole) have topped 325 since. I earned the first of six All-Star Game berths and would have sported a better than 17-11 record had the offense, which was unusually strong for an Indians club of that decade, not scored only 32 runs in my combined defeats.

Hitters marveled at my stuff. I was still only twenty-two years old, and nearly the entire season I was being likened to Sandy Koufax—that both of us were southpaws strengthened the comparison. I not only boasted what has been timed as the third-fastest fastball in major league history but my newfound awareness and dedication to the science of pitching allowed me to effectively mix in my curveball, slider, and changeup. And though I still led the league in walks, my control had improved to the point to which I could locate pitches within the strike zone well enough to consistently miss bats. And now I understood the importance of placing deliveries that forced ground-ball outs or double plays instead of trying to strike out everyone.

I eventually planned what I had perceived as a clever schedule for my bouts with the booze. I would drink heavily two nights after my starts then embrace a policy of total abstinence two nights before my next one so I could most effectively prepare. I figured I was clean and unaffected. And indeed I was performing well. It was a matter of denial. My drinking and drunken behavior worsened with time as it always will do with every addict. But at this point in my career I embraced the associated emotions and feelings. It made me feel happy. I was still fifteen years away from learning how alcohol was negatively impacting my brain.

Playing major league baseball provided me with an opportunity to drink and carouse without interference from Carol, which was tremendously unfair to her. There were no cell phones back then for her to call to check up on me. I could frequent the bars after road games—traveling from city to city afforded me the chance to experience plenty of variety among the establishments I visited.

During the summer I rented a house in the eastside suburb of Cleveland Heights from a doctor. I brought my family there once Debbie (then Tim when he was old enough) were out of school. When classes were in session I stayed at a downtown hotel that gave me a special rate. That is when my carousing would start up again. It was no wonder Carol left me on about five or six occasions. What is a wonder is that she continued to come back. She did because she loved me, which is quite a testament to her given the fact she was married to a man who did not know the definition of love and was incapable of genuinely reciprocating.

In 1965 my lifestyle gave me a sense of freedom, of doing my own thing. That feeling had grown stronger on the mound as well. My epiphany in Portland in 1964 had translated well at the major league level. I was still learning the scientific approach to my craft but I was finally taking responsibility for gaining information about opposing hitters then figuring out sequencing in pitch selection and ideal location. I could not always hit my targets, hence the bouts with wildness that plagued me more during some games and seasons than others. But I boasted the pure velocity on my fastball and movement on my breaking pitches to usually survive imperfect location. It was eye-opening for me to try to place a fastball in a certain spot and actually succeed.

My negative personality traits still prevented me from gaining a sense of joy in my achievements. I would never throughout my career embrace a strong belief in myself. But I was no longer handicapped by just raring back and firing my fastball or curve without any focus. My improved confidence and performance would continue throughout the 1960s and 1970. Thereafter my drinking problem became so pronounced that it affected my concentration, leading to an explosion in my walk totals and destroying my effectiveness.

Not until well after retirement and recovery in the 1980s could I take pride in or feel any satisfaction with my baseball accomplishments. Among the most memorable was my first All-Star Game appearance in 1965. I anticipated giving way to veterans and watching from the bullpen, so it came as a surprise when I was summoned into the game and pitched two innings. I took the loss but performed well. I even struck out Pete Rose and Frank Robinson (both of whom would be in the Hall of Fame had the former not gambled his certain inclusion away) and retired Pittsburgh hometown hero Roberto Clemente on a groundout.

Whether it was All-Star Game competition during which I called my own pitches or regular season battles when managers continued through 1967 to dictate my selections from the dugout, my stuff and location were challenged by the greatest hitters in the world. One mistake against sluggers such as Roger Maris, Al Kaline, Harmon Killebrew, Boog Powell, or Frank Howard and any pitcher was watching his offering sail into the bleachers.

Perhaps the most feared slugger in the American League during his day was Mickey Mantle. I barely knew who he was as an amateur player despite his superstardom as I did not follow professional baseball. He became my hero after I watched him perform with the perennially pennant-winning Yankees and learned about his greatness as a hitter during my early days as a major leaguer. So you can imagine how a man who lived for challenges felt facing Mantle when he stepped into the batter's box.

Perhaps the most memorable showdown in my career occurred on July 24, 1965. It was a Saturday afternoon at Cleveland Stadium. A rare throng of nearly fifty thousand filled the stands. And I fanned Mantle three times in a 3-0 complete-game victory. I boasted serious heat that day—one of those strikeouts of the Mick was on four straight fastballs. I understood from studying Mantle that my most effective approach was pitching him up and in. That is where I fired my heaters and he swung underneath them. Ah, the science of pitching! Two years earlier he might have sent one of my offerings to the moon. But now I was a pitcher, not a thrower.

The next day Mantle gave me the ultimate compliment as an insult. By this time in my career I had begun to collect autographs of all the great players and I certainly yearned for that of Mickey. I asked their clubhouse manager if Mantle would autograph a photo for me. He certainly did not have a short memory. He penned the words, "Fuck you, SOB . . . Mickey Mantle." My teammates got quite a kick out of it when I showed it to them. Pissing off Mantle was indeed quite flattering.

Little could anyone outside the sport have imagined that Mantle and I had more in common than baseball. His alcoholism was far more pronounced at that time in our careers than mine. And he never fully recovered. It destroyed him physically and eventually played a role in his early demise. He came to terms with it too late to save his life. The same almost happened to me. I am alive now because I finally arrested the disease—there is no cure.

It had just begun to take hold in 1965. In many ways that season set the tone for the rest of my career both personally and professionally. It was my first full year in the major leagues so it launched a lifestyle that became consistently more dangerous to me and my marriage as time marched on. It also contributed to a pattern of inconsistency as a pitcher that plagued me until I retired, more so in some years than others and certainly becoming far more pronounced as my alcoholic escapades became more frequent.

Run support—or generally the lack thereof from the Indians in the 1960s— greatly impacted my win-loss record and prevented me from winning twenty games in any season before 1970. Heck, I sported a 1.81 earned run average in 1968 yet compiled a 15-14 mark. But I sometimes crafted mediocre outings. I mostly dominated, but when I struggled I could not recover because my problems on the mound mostly affected my control and no pitcher is long for any game in which he walks batter after batter.

I began the 1965 season on a downer mostly because I took for granted that all would continue from the previous year. I was able to recognize my mental laziness and get myself back into form. I finished my first three starts with a 9.00 ERA and 11 walks in 14 innings. The eventual American League champion Twins knocked me out in the first inning. Then I found my groove and stayed in it. I did not allow more than three earned runs in any of my twenty-two outings from mid-May to early August and struck out at least ten batters in 10 of 19 starts during that stretch. My control deserted me in late summer, leading to a rise in my loss total and ERA but I finished strong.

The frequency of my struggles rose over the next two seasons and coincided with the growing number of philosophical clashes I had with Indians manager Birdie Tebbetts, who continued to insist on calling my pitches. I did not reach my peak as a pitcher until Alvin Dark arrived and allowed me to control my own destiny on the mound in 1968. One can only imagine what a still-young and sober Sam would have achieved in the years to come.

7

THE BATTLE
WITH BIRDIE

I believed with all my heart that I had earned the right to call my own pitches about the time *Sports Illustrated* splashed a photo of me, mouth wide open as I fired one to the plate, on the cover of its May 23, 1966, issue.

I had compiled a 7-1 record and 1.52 ERA by the time the most famous sports magazine in America went to print and I had earned my first major national recognition. I had led the Indians to their finest start in years. We had won ten straight to begin the season and held on to first place though a collapse was imminent. My only defeat had been in Baltimore, a twelve-inning grinder during which I must have thrown about two hundred pitches. Pitchers in the modern era are often removed from games when they reach one hundred pitches—I had thrown twice that many. I felt frustrated and angry that my manager continued to dictate my pitch selection when I was working my butt off in a four-hour game trying to get us a win. Tebbetts raised the number of pitches he would call for me in a game from about 20 percent at the start of his tenure to perhaps 70 percent. Joe Adcock, who took over the club in 1967, selected about half my pitches until I got into trouble. Then he often left the dugout with the excuse that he had to go to clubhouse to get tobacco (he chewed enormous amounts during the games). That took him off the hook—he would not make the wrong choice in a make-or-break scenario.

This is when I started calling pitches from the mound. I established a signal system for the catchers if Adcock called pitches I did not want to throw. I periodically turned away from this process when I lost confidence in myself. In addition, knowing that my infielders could see the catcher's signals, I forgot they could not see me changing them by swiping my chest, waist, or leg, thereby adding or subtracting numbers in the catcher's sequencing signals. This proved damaging to our defense because the infielders needed to know what I was throwing to best position themselves based on the tendencies of hitters.

The Baltimore debacle was the proverbial straw that broke the camel's back. Following my removal after the twelfth inning, I stomped into the clubhouse and called general manager Gabe Paul, who was watching the game from home. I told him that I would refuse to work if Tebbetts continued to call my pitches from the dugout. I would simply walk off the mound even if I were pitching like Cy Young and Sandy Koufax all rolled into one. I never said another word about it. Tebbetts was fired in mid-August. Later that year Indians beat writer Russ Schneider sidled up next to me on a plane and informed me of a rumor that I had said to Paul it was either Tebbetts or me—one of us had to go. That was certainly quite an exaggeration, which I explained to Schneider.

The bottom line is that the dismissal of Tebbetts, a nice person with whom I simply had professional differences, did me little good. He was replaced by George Strickland, who left in 1967 in favor of Adcock, my former Indians teammate, roommate, and hunting partner. Both continued the policy of calling my pitches. I felt frustrated and helpless.

I had evidence that the practice was hindering rather than aiding my effectiveness. California Angels standouts Jim Fregosi and Bobby Knoop even told me so over a dinner we all had together. They said their team had rather easily stolen the pitch signals from their dugout and therefore knew what offerings were on the way to the plate. They joked about it with each other during games. It was not difficult to understand. Signs are tough to pick up when the catcher is putting down fingers between his legs. They are much easier to decipher when flashed by the manager from the dugout then relayed from the catcher to the pitcher. The signs are not only easier to see, but the opposing players are provided more time to interpret them.

One example that refutes the alleged issues critics had with allowing me to call my own pitches occurred on June 23, 1968, after new Indians manager Alvin Dark gave me free reign. The team was on a hot streak fueled by one of the best and deepest pitching staffs in baseball history. We had taken three straight from eventual World Series champion Detroit to move within six and one-half games of first place and were playing the second game of a doubleheader before a rare large crowd of forty-four thousand at Municipal Stadium. I was rolling merrily along with a shutout through four innings and would have been out of the fifth had shortstop Larry Brown not extended it with an error.

Up to the plate stepped Dick Tracewski, who was batting .192. I had since 1964 gained the knowledge of two concepts through trial and error. I understood that if you throw a pitch inside, the next one should be low and away. I also learned the value of changing speeds despite the velocity on my fastball, which is how I developed an exceptional changeup, far better than the strong one I had in my amateur days. It was another one of those pitches in my repertoire that Reggie Jackson considered the best in the game. I knew that if I threw a change low and away, then jammed hitters with fastballs, they would either swing under it or would make contact inside the barrel of the bat.

These were all factors that came into play when I faced Tracewski with two runners on base. Those who complained I could always simply blow weak hitters away with fastball after fastball soon had another thing coming. An off-speed pitch would have worked a lot better than three straight heaters, the last of which Tracewski sent over the fence for a three-run homer that cost us the game. The pitch was at chest level, about the only place a high-ball hitter like him could have blasted it. I was struggling with my curve that day and that was the result. Two days later a media report claimed I tried to challenge Tracewski with a changeup and the story was taken as truth, fueling the fire of those who illogically supported managers calling my pitches. Never mind that I had compiled the lowest ERA and WHIP (walks and hits to innings pitched) rate of my career in 1968 when Dark allowed me to take responsibility for pitch selection on the mound.

Yet the Tracewski home run was most remembered when the debate raged over my pitch calling. That reflects a lack of knowledge, poor understanding, and faulty memory. Another example of the latter arose during my time as counselor for the Toronto Blue Jays. Their coach Gene Tenace, who had been a decent power hitter during his playing days, sometimes good-naturedly taunted me about how he owned me as a hitter. He bragged about how he blasted one of my fastballs over the fence at Shea Stadium where the Yankees were playing while their ballpark was being renovated in 1974. I was racking my brain trying to remember this majestic blow but I remained in good humor about it.

Soon I was accompanying the Jays on a flight from Detroit to Cleveland, where I knew a couple statisticians who looked up his record against me. Not only had he never homered, but his career batting average with yours truly on the mound was a dismal .135 with many strikeouts. So much for Tenace owning me. Now the ribbing was directed toward him. I handed Jays manager Cito Gaston the statistics on a piece of paper in the clubhouse. Gaston was always up for a friendly joke or tease. He summoned Tenace to the middle of the room and told him to talk a bit more about his dominance of one Sam McDowell.

Gaston then stopped him cold to read off the numbers in front of all his team-mates: Case closed.

Tenace was not the only fabricator—or at least hitter with poor recollection. I heard quite often stories from players who never even faced me claiming at dinners and special events they had taken me deep. It was all in good humor, of course. It is the kind of bragging common among guys post-retirement and it's all in fun. I sometimes find the teasing rather entertaining despite the obvious falsehoods. Do not misunderstand—I often did make mistakes on the mound and sometimes a hanging curve or changeup was slammed for hits or even soared over the fence. But many of the claims do not match reality. I cannot blame those who utter such nonsense. I am victimized on occasion by a faulty memory as well. The longer retired the better we performed?

Speaking of untruths, that Tebbetts did not trust me to call my own games did not jibe with what he was saying in public. He told *Sports Illustrated* in the 1966 cover story that I had a good idea of how to pitch and that I was destined for greatness. He compared me favorably to Koufax, offering rightly that I had accomplished more as a pitcher at the age of twenty-two than had the future Hall of Famer. Tebbetts even praised my concentration, which certainly would raise questions about his insistence on not allowing me to empower myself on the mound as well as his reputation for being an effective psychologist as a manager. It had nothing to do with age. Other young hurlers with far less expe-rience than me were calling their own pitches. I considered it not only insulting but a handicap to performance. Many years later it was brought to my attention that perhaps his need to take credit for making me a Hall of Famer was more important than zeroing in on any of my actual problems. He knew I had fantastic talent, much better than he had seen in his half-century or so in baseball.

My frustration with this lack of trust in me to dictate selection reached a peak in 1966 and 1967 that indeed hampered my ability to win, as did a stun-ning lack of run support that I never complained about because I realized my position-player teammates were trying their best. I knew the club was strug-gling financially, attendance was bad, and there was the possibility that owner Gabe Paul and his replacement Vernon Stouffer would move the franchise out of Cleveland. The Indians of that era felt compelled to trade away high-priced players—even before the advent of free agency—to survive.

I stuck up for my teammates when they were criticized for weak hitting. Tigers ace and legendary scamp Denny McLain once stated that he could relax pitching against the Indians. That raised my ire to such an extent that I asked Dark if he could alter the rotation to allow me to start against McLain. Dark once told reporters that if he needed to win one game he would have me on the mound. Given the talent of that Cleveland rotation I considered it quite a compliment.

The distinct lack of offense certainly hindered one of the most dominant pitching staffs in baseball. Hitters dreaded coming to Cleveland to face the likes of Luis Tiant, Sonny Siebert, and Sam McDowell in a series. In 1968 we boasted only two hitters with more than ten home runs. I know 1968 was considered the Year of the Pitcher, but that was ridiculous. We had some decent power hitters such as Fred Whitfield, Leon Wagner, and an aging Rocky Colavito in 1965 but all of them were soon gone and we were left through the rest of my time in Cleveland with poor offensive talent. We would joke in spring training about our destiny as a last-place club. But we always played with pride and grit. The Indians boasted a fine hitter or two in those years such as third baseman Max Alvis, who joined me on the American League All-Star team in 1965, but never enough of them. The opposition often pitched around Alvis because our lineup provided him little protection.

We were usually out of the pennant race by Memorial Day but we certainly enjoyed the ride, as did most teams. Baseball players, particularly in that era, loved playing jokes on one another. One of the best perpetrated by our veteran pitcher Stan Williams nearly backfired. We had arrived in Kansas City for the 1967 season opener against the Athletics (the Royals did not arrive until 1969) and were staying at the downtown Muehlebach Hotel. Williams and I visited a store across the street that sold gadgets such as exploding cigars and hand buzzers that were perfect for practical jokes. He bought a rubber gorilla mask and I bought a monster mask with the plan of playing a trick on Tiant, who could be easily frightened.

We found out what room Tiant was occupying and knocked on his door with our masks on. "Who's there?" asked Luis with obvious apprehension. "Telegram for Mr. Tiant," replied Williams in an altered voice. We heard the chain being lifted, then Tiant cracked the door just a bit. Williams kicked it wide open, growled, and raised his arms like a monster. Little did he know because he could not see down through the mask that Tiant had grabbed a very real gun and was pointing it right at his stomach. Fortunately Tiant finally recognized Stan's voice and did not pull the trigger.

Opening Day was special for every team in baseball but particularly those that understood clearly they would not be hanging around for the pennant race. That included the Indians throughout my career. We could always expect a huge crowd at Municipal Stadium, which could hold seventy thousand fans. But it was almost always cold in early April no matter where we played. I recalled a 1963 opener in Minneapolis when snow was blown away by a helicopters then gasoline was sprayed on the infield and lit to thaw out the dirt. On the bus to the stadium I listened to our hitters talking about how it hurt their hands to hit jam jobs in freezing temperatures. That pumped me up—I could not wait to fire my 100 mph heater inside and create some of that sting. I would grease myself with a gel called "atomic balm" that boasted body-heating chemicals then put on the long johns I used for hunting in the winter. I struggled in some of my opening day starts because I was not yet in the groove, but at least I stayed warm.

I knew I had to pitch well to win with the Indians. Our camaraderie, as well as the determination exhibited by my teammates, motivated me to keep my mouth shut about the lack of run support. But it certainly did not result in a victory total that befit my performance. I did, however, take a step back in 1966 and 1967, mostly due to frustration over how I was being handled. I sported a mediocre 9-8 record in 1966 with an ERA that had climbed nearly a point from the previous year.

Baseball players are forced to endure quite a bit of pain—it is part of the game. Those who cannot overcome it do not last long. And occasionally they must play through pain that weakens effectiveness. I experienced significant elbow soreness in 1966 that altered my delivery. The same scenario the following year resulted in frequent cortisone shots. Then in 1971 twenty-four cortisone shots as well as lidocaine to dull the pain allowed me to take the mound and avoid surgery for a shoulder problem. I later learned this was the most dangerous approach an athlete could take because it threatened to destroy his arm, hip, shoulder, whatever. But back then none of us, including the doctors, knew any better.

I suffered through my worst season to date in 1967 with a 13-15 mark and 3.85 ERA. That opposing hitters were catching on to stealing signs was obvious. My hits-to-innings-pitched ratio soared when I pitched for Adcock. My season with him was the only one from 1965 to 1970 in which I did not lead the American League in strikeouts or make the American League All-Star team.

I vividly recall one game against the Angels in 1967 that helped prove the point that I performed better when left to my own devices. I was pitching a shutout through six as we hung on to a 1-0 lead for dear life. I allowed successive singles to start the seventh inning, then Sims glanced from behind the plate to the dugout for another pitch call from Adcock. But he had bolted to the clubhouse for some chewing tobacco. I was happily free to extricate myself from the jam without his interference. And I did. I earned the complete-game victory.

What I perceived as a bit of overmanaging likely even cost me a major league record. The date was September 18, 1966, but I remember it like it was yesterday. We were in Detroit, which boasted a tough lineup featuring the likes of Bill

Freehan, Al Kaline, Willie Horton, and Mickey Stanley. My mound opponent was McLain, who in 1968 became the last thirty-game winner in baseball history and would soon thereafter gain a reputation as an angry flake who poured ice water over the heads of sportswriters he did not like. Heck, there was one writer in particular in Cleveland I clashed with but I never dumped ice water on his head.

Anyway, I had my best stuff that Sunday afternoon. All my pitches were working. I struck out nine batters in the first three innings and racked up fourteen through six. I was on pace for twenty-one, which would still be a record today. I seemed destined to at least break what was then the all-time major league mark of eighteen in a nine-inning game. I told Strickland that my arm felt a little stiff but I was fine to continue for at least another inning or two. He was taking no chances. Explaining later that as an interim manager he did not want to be known as the man who ruined the career of a brilliant young pitcher over a potential record, Strickland removed me from the game. I did not even get the win. Reliever John O'Donoghue blew my 5-1 lead, then Tiant rescued the victory in extra innings.

Interference from managers, as well as my own weaknesses, had begun to prevent me from reaching my potential. That was too bad because I was starting to receive some recognition, which meant a lot to a narcissist like me, though the *Sports Illustrated* article served as much to further my reputation as a flake—as left-handers are supposed to be according to baseball legend— as it did to praise my rise as a pitcher. I was portrayed as a guy who would say anything at any time and contradict myself, such as when I said I needed to beat a team in my mind before I could beat them in the field then added that I could not win if I was confident and that I had to be scared to death to perform well.

Such comments left readers scratching their heads. I often used the wrong word or phrase even when explaining factual data I had learned. What I was trying to explain was that visualizing fear helped me remove that fear and relax, thus allowing me to free my mind and develop a plan of attack. Sometimes my explanations came out wrong.

I was not trying to confuse anybody. Some in the media claimed I simply stated what they wanted to hear because I believed they were going to write whatever they wanted anyway. But that was only true of writers for whom I had little respect and who did not write truthfully about me, particularly *Cleveland Plain Dealer* beat writer Bob Dolgan, with whom I often clashed. When I told *Sports Illustrated* in a 1970 article that I sometime spoke untruthfully to reporters I was referring specifically to him. I did not like that Dolgan offered opinions in his stories, claiming to know what players were thinking rather than just stating what happened and getting quotes. It was a trend that had begun with some in the media at that time and has worsened in the modern era. The obvious motivation is that it stirs up controversy that results in greater readership and, in today's modern technology, more clicks. But Dolgan was certainly unpopular among my teammates, two of whom refused to speak with him at all. If he were among a bevy of reporters asking questions, they would simply refuse to be interviewed until he had left the clubhouse.

Criticism based on ignorance bothered me during my career. Often radio announcers and newspaper journalists who had no idea that managers such as Tebbetts and Adcock were calling my pitches complained on the air or in print about pitch selection for which I was not responsible. Neither the criticism nor the pitch calling was doing me any good. They both gave me an opportunity to condemn someone else when I failed. I could heap the blame on them. Such was certainly the case early in my career. Then when I gained an understanding of the science of pitching, I was still handcuffed. I could use my newfound knowledge in regard to location but I was not allowed to decide what pitch would be most effective in particular situations. And many in the media were unaware of this.

Dolgan and I always had a contentious relationship. Even after what should have been typical post-game interviews he had this habit of trying to think for me. That mindset continued in his writing. He would type up columns that made it clear he was seeking to explore my mind and making assumptions about what was going on inside my head. I did not believe that is what the readers wanted. They did not crave speculation. They sought the facts. I recall one *Cleveland Press* sportswriter after a Saturday afternoon game running frantically into the clubhouse seeking out my pitching mate Gary Bell to verify a quote. That was the kind of approach players respected and appreciated. The rule of the day was to write what happened and allow the readers to visualize it.

I understand that times changed as soon as all games were televised. But truth still matters, and hypothesizing the thoughts of an athlete is not truth. Dolgan was ahead of his time in constantly offering his opinion not as a columnist but as a beat writer. There is a difference. Quite often, at least in my case, he was wrong. And when I challenged him he would simply shrug his shoulders and claim it was up to the readers to decide.

That nearly led to a physical confrontation. One night I was particularly upset with a published report he wrote about me and my pitching. We nearly came to blows at a local bar (both of us were sober at the time). Though it was considered bad form for beat writers to go to bars the players they covered often frequented, he did on occasion to try to get a scoop. I got up in his face to express my anger and he grabbed my coat lapel. I swung him around and asked if he wanted to step outside. The fight never happened. I walked out the front door and waited for him. He walked out the back door and ran home. So much for barroom brawls. The drama peaked then died just as quickly.

By that time in my career my inability to partake in moderation did often result in a drunken stupor or physical altercation. I have been arrested twelve times in my life and never been convicted of a crime. In nearly all cases the police simply sat me down in the chief's office and flooded me with coffee. I sometimes spent one night in a cell. Both the public and I were fortunate that my three DUIs did not result in accidents that caused injury or even fatalities. On one occasion my backtalk to an arresting officer led to consideration of charges for public drunkenness and disturbing the peace. But I was given a break, which has been par for the course for celebrities forever.

The difference during my career—before social media and paparazzi—was that it was easier to keep arrests hush-hush. The Indians worked to do just that. Such was the case after my first arrest in 1967 when Adcock managed the club—and this is ironic because when I was Adcock's roommate during his one season as a player in Cleveland, we carried a fifth of whiskey in an attaché case—he warned me in no uncertain terms that he better not see any evidence of me drinking. On that fateful day in spring training I had remained back in Tucson while most of the team traveled to Mexico for an exhibition game. I became so snockered that I fell asleep on a table in a bar we often visited. Since I was only a periodic drinker at the time the bar owners did not recognize me. So they called the police. I was unaware the police knew who I was so I tried to hide my identity in the fear that it would reach the papers. I told them I was a laborer.

No dice—the cops stuck me in a cell and called the Indians, who dispatched the media director to bail me out. I was so out of it that I thought he'd also been arrested and blurted out, "They got you too, huh?" The team did the same sort of thing on other occasions as my drinking worsened. They protected their celebrity pitcher and the club from embarrassment.

I could not maintain an ideal relationship with the media, which during my career promoted the notion that the reason managers felt the need to dictate pitch selection was that I lived for challenges and that, for instance, if I knew I could strike out a weak hitter by blowing a fastball by him I would throw a changeup instead. The inference was that I found pitching boring if I simply fired heaters by everyone. But that was simply untrue. I had come to understand nearly from the moment I stepped onto a minor league mound that I could not get away with unleashing nothing but fastballs to professional hitters. Perhaps there were times when a well-placed fastball would have resulted in a strikeout, but having confidence in my ability to place a fastball or any other pitch in a specific place was beyond my belief system. I could eventually fire pitches to specific spots but my self-assuredness on the mound would come and go, thereby forcing me to try to outguess hitters. Interestingly this was part of the effect of my drinking that I thought I was controlling by not drinking two days before a start. But it was not because I was seeking to challenge myself at the expense of my team.

That was especially true in the major leagues. If I thought—after Dark took over in 1968 and gave me the freedom to call my own game—that based on pitch selection I could strike out a weak hitter with nothing but fastballs, I threw nothing but fastballs. But it is rare when any pitcher does not have to mix in breaking balls or something off-speed even to weaker batters. I understood that a "fastball-only" approach would be disastrous against the vast majority of big leaguers. They were simply too quick with the bat, and I knew from very painful experience that hitters who saw nothing but 100 mph fastballs tended to send them back soaring over the outfield fence at 110 mph.

And keep in mind that though pitch count was not a thing in the 1960s, I was probably averaging about 160 pitches per start and often won games in which I threw at least 170. I recall one victory at the front end of a doubleheader in Detroit after which I was told that I unleashed over 200 pitches. I lost so much weight from perspiration that Dark sent me home rather than have me accompany the team to Chicago.

Fortunately, as hitters were quite aware, I got stronger and faster as each game progressed. It was known that if you were to get to McDowell, it would be in the first three innings. If not I would gain confidence and sharpen location and become stronger. I was so conscious of getting hitters out that I pitched tentatively in the first couple innings. Once past the third I was relaxed and confident in my pitching. That made a world of difference.

But it didn't stop folks from complaining. Veteran catcher Del Crandall asserted that I wanted to throw my changeup too much. He claimed I was not as impressed with my fastball as opposing hitters were overwhelmed by it. That was true to the extent that my self-doubt and fear resulted in me underrating my talent in general. But I had discovered by trial and error that I achieved my greatest successes when I mixed in my entire repertoire and used what I had learned in 1964 and beyond about changing speeds, locating, and taking advantage of hitter weaknesses. And there seemed to be great confusion among players about my pitch selection after Dark allowed me the opportunity to actually own it. Super-slugger Reggie Jackson opined that I had the greatest fastball, curveball, slider, and changeup in the sport but that he did not mind hitting against me because our battles were strength against strength—fastball pitcher versus fastball hitter. So what was it? Was I throwing too many fastballs or not enough? Nobody could figure it out.

I have been told by serious baseball fans that when I pitched they loved the *mano y mano* battles because they all knew what I was going to throw to the likes of Mantle or Horton or Jackson. But I must admit that I cheated a bit with Reggie and would drop down to throw sidearm so his right knee would buckle.

I understood where Jackson was coming from when he said he liked to face me because it was going to be strength against strength. But when I told the media that I lived for challenges, I did not mean it the way it was interpreted. I would not throw pitches I believed had a greater chance of getting pounded simply for the sake of a challenge. I did not want to try to outguess hitters. I preferred to learn their tendencies, their strengths, and their weaknesses and then attack them based on that information. The science of pitching that was ingrained in me after my spring-training demotion in 1964 had an impact for seasons to come. Pitchers are best served with a short memory, and I did from pitch to pitch. But I always remembered getting clobbered before my professional awakening and did not want to relive that. So I was determined to pitch scientifically. If critics interpreted that as overthinking, so be it. I knew in my heart and mind that it was the best approach for me.

Eventually the outside noise became maddening. I threw myself into every endeavor that piqued my interest. I opened a family billiard parlor in Pittsburgh called Jack and Jill Cue and Cushion. I tried to learn the guitar. Both ventures had me thinking about my eventual retirement despite the fact that when those businesses were revealed publicly in 1966 I was just twenty-three years old. When I told reporters that I could just as well have chosen another career, I was speaking the truth. I began building miniature ships in bottles. I had long before started a gun collection that grew to around forty-five pieces. Because I could not put back together a lever-action rifle, I went to a gunsmithing school near Pittsburgh. I was not interested in bluing a gun or learning how to temper steel to a certain strength but I did learn how to fix guns. And of course, I was increasingly embracing my other hobby—drinking.

It is no wonder that I wanted to get away from baseball after my starts had been completed. It is also not surprising that I remained in that alcoholic fog, that malaise that continued to plague me. From about 1966 to 1968 I drank periodically, staggering my bouts with booze to prevent it from wrecking my starts. But I more often drank now to get inebriated. It was a temporary escape from reality, and though I was not out getting smashed nightly by any means, I was becoming a nastier drunk.

Freedom of choice and peak performance were right around the corner. A year of sobriety would follow before the grip of alcoholism destroyed my career and almost my life.

8

DARK BRINGS LIGHT

Three weeks had passed in spring training 1968. New Indians manager Alvin Dark summoned me into his office for a private chat. Little did I imagine I would leave the room with a feeling of career freedom. He informed me that, unlike my previous big-league skippers he was going to allow me to dictate my own pitch selection.

Finally!

Another benefit of the Dark hire was new pitching coach Jack Sanford, who had just retired after a long career that included a 19-win season in Philadelphia that earned him National League Rookie of the Year honors and a 24-7 record for the Giants that placed him second in the Cy Young Award balloting. Sanford had recently spent three years with the Angels as a teammate of Jim Fregosi and Bobby Knoop. They knew all about the drawbacks of signaling my pitches from the dugout, the ease with which they'd been stolen, and the weak position it left me in on the mound.

Joe Adcock should have known as well—he was a teammate of all of them in California. But he was the man *calling my pitches* as manager of the Indians in 1967. That it was my worst season was no coincidence. Sanford had learned what Adcock had not. And he was determined to follow Dark's lead and allow me to call my own pitches. He would also help me chart my course against the opposition du jour by going over the individual hitters. We would talk about the best approach against each as peers. It was the relationship between coach and pitcher for which I had yearned for years.

Only once did Dark call a pitch for me. It was a crucial situation during the opening series of the 1968 season against the Angels and he had a strong feeling, which I did not mind. It was the first inning, two on and two out, when dangerous power-hitter Don Mincher stepped to the plate. I had run the count to 3-2 and felt tempted to fire a fastball because it was my best control pitch and I knew I could not walk in a run. But Dark called for a curveball. He understood that I struggled to throw strikes with my hook but he had more confidence in me than I had in myself. Self-assuredness, even after all those years in the big leagues, was still not my strong suit. Mincher was definitely not expecting what ballplayers call the Uncle Charlie. It buckled his knees. In the immortal words of legendary Detroit Tigers announcer Ernie Harwell, he stood there like the house on side of the road and took a called strike three. I will never forget the look I got from Mincher as I walked off the mound. His mouth was agape and his eyes, wide as bowling balls, watched me all the way to the dugout. I felt a tremendous sense of pride. I could have jumped with joy if it would not have embarrassed me in front of the fans. (In that same game I hit Mincher in the face with a fastball. He once expressed the belief that I felt worse about it than he did. That is certainly possible. I remember visiting him in the hospital. He missed the next two weeks of the season.)

Pitching for Dark allowed me to see the light. I embarked on the finest run of my career to date after growing accustomed to the added responsibility. My earned run average dropped to under 2.00 on May 21 and remained there the rest of the season. From that date until late August I never allowed more than three earned runs in a game. I struck out 40 batters in 27 innings during one three-game winning streak and 40 more in 24 innings in another three-game run.

I knew I needed to keep runners from crossing the plate because my teammates certainly were not doing so. Not only was it the Year of the Pitcher, when scores were so low that major league baseball lowered mounds the next season to increase offensive production, but my team was among the weakest offensively in the sport. From late April through Independence Day, the Indians averaged just two runs per game in my starts. It is no wonder I compiled only a 15-14 record that year despite a 1.81 ERA that ranked among the best in baseball history. Though Major League Baseball Commissioner Bowie Kuhn denied it, I was and am to this day certain they also made the balls livelier in 1969.

Victories were hard to come by but not a good time off the field. My desire to live a celebrity lifestyle had been fulfilled, which was certainly an unfair reality to my wife Carol, who tried to limit my drinking when I was home because she cared about me. Her admonitions proved far weaker than my narcissism. But when I was traveling with the Indians, the road was my playground. I drank and womanized. I was not alone in my unfaithfulness though in all the teams I played with it was a rarity and the promiscuity was nothing like what some in the media depicted, but a few of us tried.

The baseball routine, however, was conducive to it. We were young men who were relatively attractive. We could frequent bars or clubs well into the night—it was not all that hard to avoid team curfew cops—and sleep in with or without our so-called sexual conquest until noon if we desired. There were certainly enough women who fawned upon athletes to go around. Among them were stewardesses who traveled as we did and stayed in the same hotels. I had many chances but often preferred to get drunk, thus ruining any tryst. Lord knows I tried but drinking and drunkenness proved far more important than the skirt.

Hanging out with celebrities also bolstered my sagging ego. We had several who would join our workouts or just spend time with us. Among them was Bob Hope, a Clevelander and minority owner of the Indians. Fellow legendary comedian Jerry Lewis hung out with us after shows in town. He even showed off some pretty impressive skills in the batter's box and on the mound. I got a picture of him clowning around with me in the clubhouse after a workout. Another celebrity who visited was Chuck Connors, star of the TV western *The Rifleman* and friend of Dark. Connors definitely knew his way around athletic venues. He played one season as a first baseman with the Cubs after a short career with the NBA Boston Celtics.

I also met film stars at the Old Tucson, a studio located in an area west of Tucson where we held spring training. Among them was Paul Newman, who in 1967 was filming a western titled *Hombre*. A former minor league teammate Paul Gleason, who went on to play unsavory characters in such movies as *Trading Places* and *The Breakfast Club*, often accompanied us to movie studios when we visited Los Angeles. I visited Gleason during my short stint with the Yankees while he was acting in a Broadway play.

A couple times in New York I dined at the legendary Toots Shor restaurant with Jackie Gleason among the visitors. He was a sports fanatic. I considered myself a fine pool player but I made the mistake of challenging Gleason, who had starred alongside Newman in a film about the game called *The Hustler*. He was among the best amateur players I'd ever seen. And that is saying something, considering I owned a family pool hall in which the likes of Willie Mosconi and Minnesota Fats thrilled patrons with exhibitions as did many of the local Pittsburgh greats.

Diversions help many players survive the 162-game grind. During the 1969 season I teamed with "mod" power-hitting outfielder Hawk Harrelson, who had arrived in Cleveland that year, to recite the legendary "Who's on First?"

routine made famous by Abbott and Costello. We nailed it. We filmed our bit, which would often be shown by Harrelson years later during rain delays after he became a color analyst on White Sox broadcasts.

The celebrity lifestyle certainly tested my morality and I often failed that test. Alcoholism played a significant role because it impaired the judgment needed to make a principled choice. Early in my career I stayed true. But my desire to challenge myself, the notion that I could achieve anything, combined with my narcissism, led me to frequent infidelity that I perceived as personal triumphs. Sometimes I was too drunk and would fall asleep after accompanying a young woman back to the hotel. Depending on the stage of my alcoholism, I yearned to be known as a great lover. I was not interested in the more typical barflies. I was into real beauties because they fed my self-esteem. I had affairs with two movie stars, one of them a big name who will not be identified here. I remained friends with one of them after my recovery. I shared dinner in California with her and her husband, a successful music producer who did a lot of work with Sonny and Cher. He invited me to the studio to watch them record albums. I also had a rendezvous with one of Dean Martin's backup singers.

I befriended a bevy of beautiful, sophisticated women who were not household names, such as a college professor and financial advisor. Often I began drinking at a bar and one of the single ballplayers would follow me. I would get so drunk that I could not continue in the social situation and the teammate would take the women home instead.

One time in Baltimore I met a woman at a restaurant while eating and drinking. I was so plastered I could not perform as a man should when I took her to the hotel. She simply left. I called her on our next road trip and she agreed to meet me in New York. I bought her dinner and drinks after a game but again got smashed. By the time we got to the lobby I needed a teammate to help me into my room. He left with my date and I never heard from her again.

The concept of love and of being a lover escaped me. How could I be loyal to Carol Ann when my first loyalty was to my narcissism? I had been married to her for several years. She loved a man incapable of loving her back. Her anger and frustration grew. I made promise after promise to her that I would stop drinking but I never kept my word. In the late 1960s we would negotiate my alcohol intake. She wanted me to drink only at home as she was frightened to death I'd get hurt or hurt someone else in my drunken state. Sometimes I tried to get on the wagon but I would eventually hop back off again. Little could I have imagined back then her reaction had I come clean about my infidelities on the road.

What Carol could not do with me my manager did in 1969. Dark sat me down during spring training and spoke to me in a fatherly tone. He demanded nothing from me. But he knew after spending the 1968 season with me that I had a worsening alcohol problem. So he challenged me to take a year off from drinking. I promised him I would. And I kept that promise. Not a drop of booze passed my lips from that moment until the worst year in Indians history since 1915 had mercifully ended.

I cannot claim my sobriety either aided or hindered my performance on the mound in 1969. After all, I had remained to that point a periodic drunk who maintained a schedule of boozing that kept me sober leading up to and through my scheduled starts. But one can cite the best control of my career as evidence that abstinence had a positive effect. My 3.2 walks per innings pitched ratio was easily my finest before or after, and I managed an 18-14 record with another poor offensive club.

Among the defeats we registered was one in mid-September when my temper got the best of me in Baltimore against the soon-to-be American League champion Orioles. I was going after my seventeenth win, but I was trailing 3-1 in the sixth inning when I confronted umpire Larry Barnett after throwing a 3-2 slider down the middle of the plate to my former teammate Chico Salmon. Barnett had been squeezing me all day. I had complained several times about his strike zone and my anger finally boiled over. I walked toward Barnett and had to be restrained by teammates. He ejected me from the game, walked to the mound and said, "Give me the ball, punk." I wheeled around and tried to fire it over the 109-foot stands and out of the park. I nearly succeeded. It landed three rows from the top. My reply to Barnett? "Go get it, you son of a bitch."

Orioles players spent the following days in batting practice trying to heave baseballs to where I did but to no avail. Some even used fungo bats in an attempt to reach the spot. No dice. Baltimore manager Earl Weaver finally took notice and ordered his players to stop under the threat of a $100 fine. That was big money back then. I recall that my mound opponent on that fateful afternoon was Mike Cuellar, who later became one of my friends and a golfing buddy in Florida.

My insecurity and the effects of the alcohol sometimes reared its ugly head and I would revert to guessing on the mound instead of taking control and throwing what I believed to be the best pitch to a particular batter. But years later I finally gained some appreciation for what I'd achieved in my career. I recognized the heavy burden that had been placed on my shoulders in 1969, and not only from the pressure of maintaining sobriety. The trading of rotation-stalwart Sonny Siebert and sudden struggles of Luis Tiant left Sudden Sam as the only premier pitcher on the staff. It was no wonder we finished 62-99. I was not carrying a monkey on my back. It was more like a gorilla, but I rose to the occasion.

Yet to this day I do not know how I achieved that. I had stopped drinking, albeit temporarily, but I still lived in the same alcoholic fog that had plagued me all my life. I remained in a low-level depression. I could have explained to Dark when he asked me to stop drinking in 1969 that I had not allowed it to affect my performance so I should be free to do whatever I wanted off the field. But there was no demonizing or condescension in his tone or approach to what he was asking of me so I felt compelled to comply.

Perhaps if I had been a different man the year of abstinence would have inspired me to kick the drinking habit for good. But I was still plagued by depression, insecurity, and poor self-esteem. The early days of drunkenness in the mid-1960s that had put me in a happier place and allowed me to feel normal were slipping away. When the 1969 season concluded, I not only picked up where I left off but began to lose control of my drinking in frequency and moderation. After my last start I bought a six-pack of beer and began drinking it in the clubhouse. I will never forget the look of disappointment from Dark when he walked by and realized my abstinence was over.

At that point Dark met with Sanford, who agreed to accompany me to bars whenever we were on the road to limit my alcohol intake. Little did I know at the time Dark was simply trying to protect me, especially since I had become an angry drunk who would engage in barroom brawls.

Dark cannot be blamed for me jumping off the wagon. First of all he could not be responsible for the off-the-field actions of Sam McDowell, let alone every player on his team. In addition his primary goal was to win games and keep his job. The miserable mark in 1969 placed him in the hot seat. He tried in vain to keep me on the straight and narrow following a couple of embarrassing DUIs after we broke camp. He threatened fines if he ever caught me drinking, but after three lousy outings early in 1970 he feared the ultimatum was wrecking my performance so he called me aside and gave me the green light to booze.

I returned to the scheduled drinking that allowed me to stay sober as I prepared for starts and on days I pitched and embarked on the most dominant stretch of my career. I even emerged during that period as a control pitcher, which combined with my overwhelming stuff had batters making weak contact or shaking their heads, returning to the dugout as strikeout victims. From mid-May to early August I compiled a 13-2 record, won seven straight decisions during one stretch, and averaged 2.5 walks per outing. I hurled complete-game victories without walking a batter against Boston and Minnesota, two of the most powerful offenses in the American League.

And still the media was unsatisfied. In mid-August I was again featured prominently in a *Sports Illustrated* article (though New York Jets superstar quarterback Joe Namath landed on the cover), this one painting me as an underachiever. Writer Pat Jordan compared me unfavorably to Hall of Fame pitcher Robin Roberts, who had won twenty or more games for the Phillies every year from 1950 to 1955. Jordan asserted that since Roberts could rack up such victory totals for a weak Philadelphia club I should have done the same with Cleveland.

Jordan either failed to delve further into the numbers or elected to ignore them. First of all, my peak arrived at a far younger age than that of Roberts, who was a more experienced pitcher. Second, I compiled about the same ERA during those periods in our careers despite Roberts's boasting far superior control. Third, the Phillies were not nearly as bad offensively as were the Indians of my era. They scored far more runs for Roberts than my teammates did for me, yet I never complained publicly. If I had pitched for Detroit, Boston, or Minnesota I would have won twenty several times.

Sports Illustrated cited me as stating that I lived for challenges so if I knew I could retire a batter with one pitch, I would throw a different pitch his next time to the plate. My quote, which was picked up by other media outlets, was misconstrued. I always used the best pitch in my repertoire against any batter until he proved he could hit it. But I also knew that taking the same approach with the same hitter every at-bat was a recipe for disaster because he would know what was coming. I wanted to keep batters guessing. That put me in control. Yes, I lived for challenges. But I never weakened any opportunity to retire a hitter simply for the sake of a challenge. That would not have been fair to me or my teammates.

Another focus of the article portrayed me as dishonest with the media. It listed statements I had made about my motivations as a pitcher, among them about my desire to break franchise strikeouts records set by the immortal Bob Feller. That stemmed from my first trip to Cleveland after signing with the Indians when a reporter asked me if I would like to break Feller's records and of course I said, "Yes. Who wouldn't?" The papers the following day falsely claimed I said that I signed with the Indians so I could break Feller's records, which was not at all what I meant. But that line followed me throughout my career no matter how often and vigorously I tried to debunk it.

Sports Illustrated also quoted me as admitting that I no longer cared what I told reporters. But that was only true in the case of *Plain Dealer* writer Bob Dolgan. I just did not want to mention him by name in a national publication.

One accurate claim in the article was uttered by local television sportscaster John Fitzgerald, who offered that I had been hurt earlier in my career by bad publicity and that I felt people expected too much from me so I hid behind a few conflicting remarks so I would not get hurt again. Fitzgerald called me a big kid who was afraid of getting hurt, which was true. I had grown as a pitcher but I remained very immature as a person. And early in my career, when some of those contradictory statements were made, I simply reacted to questions asked of me without thinking about how I had answered them weeks or months or years earlier. In nearly all cases I was not being dishonest.

My performance in 1970 earned me another All-Star Game nod but was not good enough for acerbic Indians radio announcer Bob Neal, whose dour personality years earlier clashed so badly with his booth partner Jimmy Dudley that they never even talked to each other on or off the air. During his time with the Indians, including when I failed twice to win my twentieth game in 1970 (despite pitching well), he claimed publicly that I had a "million-dollar arm and ten cent head." Our feud became media fodder. I retorted that Neal was unpopular for a reason.

This is not to indicate that I always performed to my potential. When you do not believe in yourself, poor performance becomes a fait accompli. I was quoted correctly in *Sports Illustrated* as saying I was more or less forced into a baseball career, never believed I was very talented, and continued to feel that way well after I had been pushed into the majors before I was ready. So when baseball insiders, media members, and fans demanded that I live up to my so-called potential, it had the opposite effect. Whatever I accomplished on the mound was never enough. That is especially true for an alcoholic. I hated the demands made of me. I rejected accountability and responsibility.

That mindset extended back to my youth. You must understand that I was never happy. I did not feel even the slightest appreciation for my achievements until after my recovery in the 1980s. I enjoyed challenges and thought overcoming them would bring me contentment. But my alcoholic personality dictated that I could never be satisfied. I had dreams early in life of being a doctor or an NFL quarterback. Given my personality, it would not have mattered. I would still have suffered from the same problems. So I looked for outside stimuli such as drinking to make me happy. What I would not understand until after I hit rock bottom and took responsibility for my well-being was that the solution was internal.

One historical baseball event added to the intrigue of the 1970 season. My run of fine performances earned me second spot in the pitching rotation at the All-Star Game in Cincinnati. What proved far more noteworthy about that game than my three shutout innings in which I allowed just one hit was the final play. The American League and National League were tied at 1-1 in the ninth inning.

Hometown hero Pete Rose was on second base when fine Cubs hitter Jim Hickman lined a base hit that was scooped up by Kansas City center fielder Amos Otis, who fired it home. My Indians teammate Ray Fosse, who was blossoming into stardom, fielded the ball on one bounce as Rose was barreling to the plate but Rose arrived a split-second before the ball. He crashed into Fosse to score the winning run. While the National Leaguers celebrated yet another All-Star Game victory during their long run of triumphs, Fosse sat on his haunches in pain.

Most interesting about all of it for me was the reaction. Many believed Fosse and I hated Rose but we did not. He had invited us to dinner the night before and was extremely gracious. Rose said he planned to slide on the play but Fosse was blocking him in front of the plate, which was true. I had no reason to doubt Rose.

A subsequent x-ray seemed to reveal nothing wrong with Fosse's shoulder. Cleveland doctors cited only a bad bruise but such was not the case. The inflammation and swelling prevented a shoulder separation and fracture from showing up on the x-ray. Fosse could barely lift his arm to catch pitches or throw the ball. But the expectation among ballplayers in that era was to play through pain. So he did not tell Dark and the manager did not ask. Fosse, who appeared destined for greatness, was never the same. He remained a decent hitter but lacked the power that marked the first half of the 1970 season.

Meanwhile, my issues, more emotional than physical, were about to take a devastating toll on my career as well. I certainly had not learned any lessons by the dawning of the 1970s. I had through the first year of that decade stopped my drinking from weakening my performance on the mound. But now it was about to destroy my career.

9

GOODBYE, CLEVELAND

His name was Tony Horton. He was a teammate of mine in Cleveland. We both had psychological problems, but they were as dissimilar as a baseball and a telephone pole.

Horton was neurotically tense; I was brazen. He gripped his bat as if trying to turn it into sawdust; I was accused of not taking my career seriously enough. He never tried to enjoy life; I tried so hard to enjoy life that I nearly ruined it. He had such an insatiable drive to succeed; I was not greatly impacted by professional success or failure. But we did have two things in common. We were both tremendously talented baseball players, and we both tried to kill ourselves.

I became familiar with Horton when he was traded to the Indians from Boston early in Boston's Impossible Dream season of 1967. The Red Sox boasted a slugging first baseman in George "Boomer" Scott, and he made Horton expendable. Nobody I met during my career worked harder at his craft than Horton. He was so determined to achieve greatness that in his own mind there was no ceiling to his potential. He could not even crack a smile rounding the bases after slugging a home run. He took extra batting practice until his hands bled. It seemed every out—and even the best hitters are retired seven out of ten times at the plate—was destined to cause him spontaneous combustion. He could have been satisfied as a very productive young contributor to an offense desperately needing the talent he could provide. He could spray line drives around the field with enough power to pile up home runs.

He began to show symptoms of a serious mental illness by 1970. I will never forget the day it all came crashing down. It was August 28, 1970. We were playing a Friday home doubleheader against the Angels. Horton was going from player to player asking them their definition of a man and if they considered him one.

Horton had held out for more money early that year, raising the ire of Indians fans who were unaware of his issues. They booed him, and it destroyed his already fragile mental and emotional state. He became so distraught that he left the team in the middle of the second game that day. Published reports claim he returned to the motel in which he was staying (though I recall him living in an apartment), got into his car that evening, and tried to slit his wrist. My understanding is that he was escorted to the airport after his departure from the team and his suicide attempt in the bathroom of his plane was thwarted by an air marshal.

I remember vividly that Horton did not leave Cleveland immediately because he asked Dark if he could speak with me before the game I was scheduled to pitch the following day. Dark informed me that Horton was experiencing severe emotional problems, which was an understatement. It was actually a breakdown. But to counsel him I had to break my usual rule of talking to nobody before a start. (Not talking to anyone allowed me to focus on the strengths and weaknesses of the hitters I'd soon be facing.)

We sat on the bench, me in my baseball underclothing and him in his street clothes (I do not recall any damage to his wrist, which leads me to believe that he had not attempted suicide the previous night) and he asked me if I thought there was anything seriously wrong with him. I said no. He kept insisting that I tell him how I handled the pressure of pitching in the big leagues—me of all people. I finally answered that even if a hitter was better than me I wanted to avoid being embarrassed. I told him I just tried to do the best I could. He sadly said he was letting everyone down. He repeated that assertion throughout our conversation.

Either way, it was fortunate he survived. But at age twenty-seven he was done with baseball. The pressure had overwhelmed him. He moved in with his father in California and never played again. I later met Tony at a restaurant when I visited Anaheim in 1971. He seemed fine. He laughed often during our conversation. It might have been the first time I'd heard him laugh.

Horton was recuperating. Meanwhile I was deteriorating. There is no exact timetable for those fortunate enough to recover from serious psychological problems. Though I had since childhood been plagued by an alcoholic personality, around the same time I dined with Horton I was realizing undeniably that I was in a losing battle with addiction. I had previously controlled it well enough to prevent it from wrecking my career, but in 1971 I began drinking myself out of baseball, out of my marriage, and into an oblivion from which I would not escape for nearly a decade.

The beginning of the end arrived with the departure of Jack Sanford as my pitching coach and confidante. He had become a very special friend who understood my issues and helped me navigate them well enough to keep me performing well. The financially strapped Indians had low-balled him in contract talks, motivating him to leave for a job managing a golf course. I offered to pay him out of my own salary, but to no avail.

Sanford was gone. He had been a guardrail that prevented me from swerving into a worsening drinking problem that threatened to endanger my career. Soon a typical alcoholic progression sent me reeling to the point of no return. I engaged in epic bouts of drunkenness that often resulted in fights and arrests that the Indians scrambled to resolve and keep secret from the media. In most cases I was the perpetrator in barroom brawls. I cannot even to this day provide a reason aside from simply wanting to be left alone to get drunk. And when someone interrupted that pursuit, I became violent.

One confrontation during that tumultuous period in my life could have been followed by my funeral. I was in a bar near the old Cleveland Arena on Euclid Avenue itching for a fight. Most often nothing came of my self-destructive tendencies during my drunken escapades but on this night I had raised the ire of the owner before I had begun to drink. During a brawl two weeks earlier I had broken most of the glassware used by the waitresses to fill drinks. The owner stood near the door that night and placed his hand firmly on my chest as I walked by. I figured he was just kidding around and continued to walk. Soon he pulled out a gun and threatened me with it. I grabbed him around the collar but he didn't pull the trigger. Quite fortunately, I proved lucky again. We eventually cooled off and sat down to talk. I did not get drunk that time but most often by 1971 I did. People told me I had a drinking problem. No! I had a stopping problem.

I put myself in dangerous situations even when I was not to blame for some kind of catastrophe. I remained naïve about the world around me, which combined with drunkenness sometimes resulted in disaster. One summer evening after a ballgame in Cleveland, I stopped at a bar and proceeded to (surprise!) get drunk. I made some rude comments to the wife of a man sitting nearby and a fight ensued. I looked up as the brawl ended and saw the bar owner pointing a gun at my stomach. He told me to get the hell out and never come back.

I thought little of the incident until the following winter when I received a phone call from two Cleveland cops with whom I was familiar. They asked to meet me in a bar near my Pittsburgh home, where they informed me that the joint in which that fight had occurred burned to the ground and witnesses claimed I was the perpetrator. The officers suggested I meet with the bar owner. I said nothing. I returned home to check my schedule and discovered that I had been back in Pittsburgh for a sports banquet on the evening of the fire. I remained in a state of shock over the whole thing so I called a friend who told me he would take care of it. He did not detail his plans but assured me that I had nothing to worry about. He was right—but I sure worried like crazy about it until then.

More than two years later after an autograph session in Youngstown somebody approached me out of the blue and asked me whatever happened regarding me and that fire. He knew something but he did not tell me much. All I understood and really cared about was that my name was never again associated with that event. To this day I do not know all the motivations but I suspect blackmail.

One could not accuse the Indians of any shady dealings during that time but I certainly struggled to find common ground in contract negotiations, particularly before the 1970 season. As usual the organization was in flux. Gabe Paul remained in an administrative capacity behind owner Vernon Stouffer but had handed general manager duties over to Alvin Dark. That Dark was being paid as manager and general manager certainly spotlighted the financial situation of a club that perennially finished near the bottom of the American League not only in the standings but in attendance.

I had problems with Paul well before 1971. He embraced a philosophy held by many team executives in the reserve-clause era during which players remained powerless and had no choice but to play through pain. Former Yankees pitcher Jim Bouton wrote humorously in his controversial 1970 book *Ball Four* about how trainers figuratively pushed players onto the field no matter what injury or level of agony they were experiencing. It was true. The idea was emphasized to players by general managers, managers, trainers, and team doctors. Paul even sent me a letter around midseason stating that major league hurlers needed to pitch through pain. He added that I was no different and it was about time I grew up and learned to push through. The mandate did not surprise me. It was his proven mantra.

During my career I sustained a variety of painful injuries common to pitchers, including strains and pulled muscles and ligaments. There were times I felt I needed to take some time off but the only solution offered to me was a cortisone shot. The pain at times reached near-excruciating levels. But the only time I was allowed to rest and heal was during the offseason. In most cases I was sent back to the mound to pitch in pain and at around 75 percent effectiveness. The problem with that scenario for me and hundreds of other players was that reduced production due to playing through pain was used in contract negotiations to cut salary.

Haggling over money was particularly stressful for Cleveland players. The Indians suffered so mightily that until Nick Mileti bought the club from Stouffer after the 1971 season, we were on the verge of being moved to New Orleans. The threat of taking the club elsewhere had been hanging over the heads of Indians fans for a decade and it was certainly not their fault. The team simply had not put a product on the field that inspired them to attend games. The result was that extracting a raise from Paul was like pulling a tooth from an enraged tiger. Never mind that I was coming off my only twenty-win season—he insisted that the team could not afford any significant raise. But I was not about to settle for a lousy contract simply because the team claimed it had no money.

So I staged a holdout into spring training. Three weeks after my teammates arrived in Tucson, I still could not convince Paul to budge. Dark called to tell me that ready or not he was penciling me in as the opening day starter because I drew the most fans. The Indians needed a big crowd for the opener since they drew very little thereafter, especially when their team was as bad as it was destined to be in 1971. Paul claimed I would ruin my arm trying to get ready for the season if I held out any longer. He convinced me that he would work out a contract with which I would be satisfied so I packed my bags, told Carol that I was leaving, and flew to Tucson to connect with Paul.

We met at the Pioneer Hotel, which just two months earlier had been devastated by a fire that killed twenty-nine people but had since been refurbished on two floors only. Later hotel personnel showed us some of the burned out floor, which was untouched to the degree you could see the chalk outlines of the different bodies from the fire. It was kind of eerie sleeping there. Later during spring training while I was asleep a fire alarm went off because of a small fire in the kitchen.

Anyway, Paul had indeed negotiated a deal by the time I arrived. He stated that he had been able to get me the $100,000 I wanted, not mentioning that it was the media that claimed $100,000 was my asking price. I had never done so. Anyway, the raise was not a raise at all. I would earn more only if I reached certain goals in walks, strikeouts, and ERA based on my 1970 season. I realized that my 1970 season would be tough to match or improve upon, but I signed. In addition, I was to receive a dime for every fan who paid to come into the stadium above my average of the previous year. That did not bode well.

There was another problem beyond the difficulty of achieving those goals: the contract was illegal (performance-based contracts were disallowed by the league). He admitted as much but (wink, wink) added that no one would find out as the contract would remain in his office safe, which he showed me. So I signed and went to work.

Soon I began experiencing an unusually high level of pain in my shoulder. I pitched seven strong innings in a victory against the defending world champion Orioles in the season opener and attributed the pain to the comparatively short amount of time I'd had to prepare for the season following the holdout. I figured my shoulder would loosen up eventually but it never did. I pitched with tremendous discomfort that entire year.

Then there was another form of discomfort. I received a call during the season from Baseball Commissioner Bowie Kuhn. He asked me to meet him the next day in his New York office. To my surprise, when I checked into the hotel I saw teammates Graig Nettles and Vada Pinson. It turned out they too had signed performance-based contracts. Kuhn withheld punishment but forced us to accept only our base salaries. The bottom line? I'd won twenty games in 1970 but did not receive a raise in 1971.

I was incensed. Indians management knew all along that the contract was against the rules—Paul admitted as much—and I suspected that he made certain the league office voided it just when the raise was about to kick in. But I could not be sure. Though Kuhn fined the Indians $5,000 for the violation, that amount paled in comparison to what the Indians saved in bonus payments. My resulting trade demand became big news. My anger at the organization proved stronger than my love for Cleveland and all the friends I had made in that city since joining the team a decade earlier. My anger at Paul was so intense, I was not thinking at all about all the friends and fans I had enjoyed throughout my career.

So I quit three days after I pitched the Indians to a defeat of California in late July, then I got suspended. Pinson and Nettles had agreed to join me in the walkout but they caved quickly for financial reasons. Though I was earning $72,000 at the time I could also not afford to sit out the rest of the season, especially if I were going to live the celebrity lifestyle to which I had grown accustomed. So I returned ten days later. But players union head Marvin Miller sided with me. He protested the comparatively measly penalty slapped on the Indians by major league baseball.

Another wrench was thrown into the works that summer. My shoulder problem worsened considerably in July. Today my injury would be treated with minor surgery or a long rest, especially given that the Indians were playing for nothing but pride by that time while compiling their worst record in eighty-seven years. But I missed just two starts and was forced right back on the mound.

Shoulder pain had been an issue since 1966. Dark informed me during spring training in 1971 that a Japanese ball club was soon arriving to play

American teams during a two-week stint. I expressed an interest in receiving a treatment that I had heard about called acupuncture. Dark explained to me that the procedure entailed little needles placed in the skin. I was all for it. The trainer of the Japanese team agreed to perform acupuncture on my shoulder. I was surprised at the immediate benefits. I pitched with little pain two days later. But the departure of our visitors precluded further acupuncture treatment and the shoulder pain eventually worsened, hampering my effectiveness that season.

One might think, examining my performance in 1971, that Dark, who was fired in late July and replaced by my old minor league manager Johnny Lipon, would have preferred I take a break and allow a young pitcher to earn some big-league experience. All the issues that stemmed from my holdout combined with my shoulder injury and an alcoholic lifestyle to negatively impact my performance, resulting in my worst year since 1963.

I failed to focus. My control deteriorated. My walk totals soared and strikeout numbers dropped. Hitters wore out a path to first base. I walked nine in successive starts in April and fell to 0-4 for the season. I walked 10 and somehow beat Washington in mid-May. I walked 33 batters over one 32-inning stretch yet won each of those starts. Such success was not sustainable. After I returned from my short absence to nurse my ailing shoulder and beat Chicago, improving my record to 12-10, I lost seven of the next eight decisions and finished the year by taking a pounding against powerful Baltimore.

During that season I had received more than twenty cortisone shots as well as lidocaine, which deadened my shoulder for short periods. I often could not tolerate the pain for more than five or six innings and was forced to leave games. Our trainer gave me extra massages and rubdowns with hot and cold towels.

Many factors contributed to my struggles on the mound in 1971. One cannot pitch hurt and angry and maintain the focus necessary to retire big-league hitters. The pain forced me to release the ball from different angles. And my alcohol addiction had worsened. I probably got drunk more often in 1971 than at any point in my career, which is quite a claim considering many of my worst moments were yet to come. It would not take a baseball savant to know, examining my 13-17 record and career-high 153 walks, that something was seriously wrong. But I remained far too immature a person to deal with any of it constructively. I had begun to lose the ability to overcome the growing number of obstacles the outside world and my own immaturity placed in my path to success. For the first time, Bad Sam was winning.

10

HELLO, MISERY

That loss to the Orioles to end the 1971 season would be my last game in a Cleveland uniform. Paul had grown weary of and frustrated with my drunken escapades and bailing me out of jail. If he had revealed that I continued to suffer from shoulder issues, he would certainly not exact a great return for a pitcher perceived as injured property. So he kept it a secret to potential trade partners. League rules stated explicitly that one team could not trade damaged goods to another unless it put into writing an acceptance of liability. I learned later that the Giants knew nothing of my injury.

By the end of that tumultuous year I was simply happy to get away from Paul. I also felt driven to gain a better understanding beyond my shoulder problems of why I struggled so mightily on the mound that season. Moreover I knew something else was wrong with me. So I delved deeper into my coursework in psychology, looking for answers that did not exist because my coursework did not address addiction. I remained years away from the realization that I was indeed an addict and that what I suffered from was a disease.

Sports psychology had aided me in building confidence in my pitching. It had the potential to bolster my levels of accountability and responsibility but my drinking thwarted that opportunity while ruining my health. Much of my motivation was to gain attention. And when I arrived in San Francisco I had a new group of teammates to try to impress. So rather than focus solely on making an impression through my pitching, I sought to do so with inebriated antics. I recall one incident with my teammates in a San Diego bar that featured a swimming pool behind glass. Pretty "mermaids" were splashing around in the pool. I was already smashed from drinking on the plane from Los Angeles so I jumped in and began swimming with the young ladies. My fellow players got quite a kick out of my exploits. I had captured their attention. Mission accomplished. My drinking was only controlled enough to keep me sober on the mound. Other than that, I was unrestrained.

A surface view indicated I remained valuable. I was a six-time All-Star. I had just turned twenty-eight years old. I was still among the hardest throwers in baseball. My poor 1971 season could be chalked up to various legitimate frustrations, such as being victimized by the team in contract dealings and an annual lack of run support. What other organizations did not realize during an era in which they could more easily hide player issues was that I was quickly deteriorating into the worst drunkard in the sport. Paul knew it. He was not about to reveal that reality in trade talks. Paul could not have swindled San Francisco general manager Horace Stoneham out of soon-to-be Cy Young Award winner Gaylord Perry and viable starting shortstop Frank Duffy by blurting out, "Oh, by the way, McDowell is a boozer prone to barroom brawling."

Perhaps I should have known a trade was coming but I had no idea until San Francisco manager Charlie Fox, with whom I had gained a friendship during spring trainings in Arizona, called to inform me. I was happy to get away from Paul and I understood that the Giants organization had a fine reputation, but though I was not at this point in my life thinking through many things, it did occur to me that being so distant from my family had its drawbacks. If I had really given it significant consideration I might have recognized that I needed to dramatically alter my lifestyle. What happened instead would send my career and marriage spiraling out of control.

And what I claimed publicly after the trade can be summed up in five words: me and my big mouth. I had no genuine reaction to the deal that sent me from Cleveland to San Francisco—my personality disorders prevented me from experiencing genuine feelings about anything practical. So instead of simply telling the media I would work to perform my best with the Giants, I allowed my uncontrolled yap to claim that I was thrilled with the move and that I was going to take them to the pennant. Given my mental and physical condition at the time, that was a boast I could not back up. My emotions affected me as well. I was devastated by the trade. I loved Cleveland and hated Paul the way a petulant child might hate a parent who punishes him.

I was justified in expecting much more run support from my new team. But that proved to be true only because the 1972 Indians remained one of the weakest hitting clubs in baseball. The once-explosive Giants had faded. The immortal Willie Mays was on his last legs and Hall of Fame slugger Willie McCovey was also aging, resulting in offense mediocrity.

Not that it would have mattered. The out-of-control Sam McDowell of 1972 could not lead any team to a pennant. There had been some doubt the previous year about whether my alcoholism adversely influenced my performance but all doubt was quickly removed soon after my arrival in San Francisco. Alcoholism reared its ugly head even before my first spring training with the Giants. I was scheduled to arrive in Arizona a month early to act in a commercial, a commitment that promised me a new car. I showed up on the set drunk and got arrested then received the star treatment from the police, who let me go. I got plastered and arrested a couple months later during spring training.

Fear also played a role in my disintegration from All-Star to struggling starter. I was scared to death from the moment the trade was announced. The Giants viewed me as a savior. They could not have predicted the depths to which I had fallen. They only knew me from spring-training games and All-Star competitions when I was at my peak. The 1-2 pitching punch of Gaylord Perry and Juan Marichal had been among the best in the sport. Now Perry was gone and Marichal had begun sliding ineffectively toward the end of his career. I was pegged as the ace of the staff. The pressure on an alcoholic such as me was unbelievable and I was in no condition to rise to the occasion. I proved to be the least-reliable performer in the starting rotation.

I don't mean to give the impression that I was getting smashed every night in San Francisco. But both my drinking and drunkenness escalated significantly. I was becoming inebriated most of the time I drank. The effects proved far more damaging to my effectiveness on the mound than it had in the past. It exacerbated my fears, self-doubt, and defensiveness. Pitchers must perform confidently, intelligently, aggressively. I was not drunk on the mound but my alcoholic lifestyle prevented me from achieving the level of focus necessary to succeed consistently.

Not that I bombed out immediately either. But even during spring training I noticed a higher degree of pain in my shoulder. I felt it every day. Often after a few weeks any discomfort that I had not worked out over the winter dissipated. Not in 1972. Moreover, that was the year of the first player strike that launched an era of battles between players and owners that lasted nearly a quarter-century. We found an amateur field to work out on during the work stoppage, which lasted about a week into the regular season. But there was no organization, no management, no trainers. I threw batting practice and did my running but there was no calisthenics, stretching, or any routine that pitchers ritualistically practice preparing for the year.

One incident from the strike remains vivid in my memory. All the players who neither lived in San Francisco nor had been joined by their families stayed in a motel south of Candlestick Park. One day we all drove over to the stadium to pick up our equipment but it was locked up. Suddenly we noticed Mays breaking the window of a door to get into the locker room for his stuff. Little did he know that someone had seen him and called the police. But the moment the police arrived to see the great Willie Mays, they left.

Despite the pain I launched my National League stint by winning my first five decisions. Granted, my strikeout totals were down and I was not exactly knocking off the beasts of the world—four of the victims were lowly San Diego, Philadelphia (twice), and Montreal. But I had walked just 15 batters in 52 innings and lowered my earned run average to 2.57 on May 10. And I was overcoming an issue that I had feared would affect me in home games: frigid temperatures and winds. It was so darn cold at Candlestick. I do not recall any game for which I did not wear long underwear even in the middle of the summer but especially at night.

By mid-May I had begun to collapse. A disturbing trend developed. The same Sam McDowell who twice allowed the fewest hits per inning in the American League was now allowing nearly one hit per inning and striking out significantly fewer hitters. I was no longer missing bats or inducing weak contact. Over the next two months I compiled a 3-7 record and 5.52 ERA, numbers that I had not been plagued with since I was twenty-year-old in 1963 and had not yet learned how to pitch.

I knew how to pitch in 1972 but internal and external forces were preventing me from turning that knowledge into an advantage. I could use my lack of familiarity with National League hitters as an excuse but that would be a lie. Had I been in a better place mentally and emotionally I could have more effectively learned their weaknesses. Rather than pitching aggressively and confidently, I was on the defensive. My physical state also played a role. My shoulder injury began to flare up again. It worsened a bit with each outing. It was causing significant pain by the second month of the season.

That became such a problem that Fox began stretching out my starts to give me an extra day or two off. I could sometimes pitch about seven effective innings in that scenario. I even finished the year with back-to-back wins. But the Sam McDowell who averaged more than thirteen complete games a year from 1964 to 1970 managed just four in 1972 and none after June 14.

Indeed, the struggles were not all my fault. The shoulder ailment that I had hoped would fully heal during the offseason began to throb again, leading to an addiction to pain pills. And the injury, of course, took a toll on my stuff. I was throwing neither as hard nor with as much bite on my curve or slider. Five consecutive poor starts in late June and July that resulted in three losses and two no-decisions with which my walk totals began to rise proved to be the last straw. I was placed on the disabled list and remained there for nearly seven weeks. I pitched better upon my return but to this day I consider my first season in San Francisco a waste. It would become the defining reality of the rest of my career.

Fox suspected by then the Indians had traded him damaged goods—not because of my drinking but rather my shoulder. But if he did not fully understand that my problems extended beyond the mound, he certainly did when a drunken Sam was arrested at Phoenix Sky Harbor Airport early in spring training the following year and charged with public intoxication. When I was pinched the cops also confiscated a bottle of pain pills they found in my possession. The police report stated I was being combative, using vulgar language, and refusing to cooperate when it was requested that I call a friend to take me home.

All true. I have been asked by those who do not understand the various stages and intricacies of alcoholism why mine often resulted in belligerent behavior and barroom brawls. What I did not know at the time but learned during my recovery is that an alcoholic or drug addict will go through different phases depending on the part of the brain most affected by the substance. Among those phases are sadness, silence, euphoria, sleepiness, anger, and feelings of being in love with any skirt in the bar. There are four levels of drunkenness before death. The first two are an attempt to remain fully functional and unnoticed. In the last two stages, the addict cannot control his or her inebriation level or conduct. There is at that point no predicting what kind of behavior will be exhibited at any time in the addict's drunken state. I lived through all the phases of intoxication and behavior. I was not always an angry drunk who acted out on that rage. But as my alcoholism became more pronounced and I became less able to control my behavior, the number of violent incidents increased.

The Giants regretted trading for me. Fox knew that Perry had won the Cy Young Award with Cleveland. The media and fans were criticizing the organization for making the deal. San Francisco had descended from Western Division champion in 1971 to a team with one of the worst records in the National League. I could not accept all the blame. Several other players, including Bobby Bonds and Marichal after Mays was traded to the Mets, did not perform as well as they had in the past. But Fox became alarmed upon learning of my arrest in Phoenix and my abuse of painkillers. He asked me privately about the latter and I replied that the shoulder injury and resulting pain necessitated the pill consumption.

All anyone could do at that point was hope for a better 1973 season. But I knew how it felt when my shoulder and arm were fine. I remembered vividly the feeling I had when I was comfortable challenging hitters. But that physical sensation and mindset on the mound had disappeared, never to return.

Fat chance I was going to rebound to any semblance of my peak. I was a mess and not just as a pitcher. Anyone who thinks living in a city such as San Francisco lured me into more deviant behavior has another thing coming. It would not have mattered where I played. My family could not join me until the kids were out of school and then they returned home a couple of months later, which left me to my own devices on the road and back in San Francisco.

Perhaps the primary reason the Giants were willing to trade Perry for me was the age difference. General manager Horace Stoneham made that claim to the media after concluding the deal. After all, I was four years younger. But there is chronological age and body age. I recall Paul defending the swap, claiming that the addition of shortstop Frank Duffy along with Perry put it over the top. It was also suggested that Perry had a younger body than mine and that his career would outlast mine. I might have resented such a comparison at the time but it proved accurate. Perry won a Cy Young Award with San Diego in 1978 and was still pitching in 1983, eight years after I had put the finishing touches on the destruction of my career.

It nearly ended two years earlier. Persistent neck and arm pain, possibly exacerbated by a change in my delivery due to the shoulder injury, motivated me to contemplate retirement in spring training 1973. Isometric exercises suggested by a doctor improved my condition enough to keep me active. But Fox had lost faith in me as a starter and moved me to the bullpen. That new role and old emotional problems combined to worsen my already lousy control. I pitched decently in spot starts but could not find the plate in relief. I walked nearly a batter per inning early in the year and again got battered when I did throw strikes. The result was a 9.00 ERA after five outings.

I found my groove in May and even earned a couple saves but the Giants had not intentionally dealt for an ailing, deteriorating, inconsistent reliever. They had traded for what they'd hoped would be a stud starter and those hopes had been dashed. So in June they sent me packing to the Big Apple. They could not even exact a player from the Yankees. All they could get for me was $50,000 in a straight cash deal.

Purchase a narcissistic alcoholic with a penchant for carousing in bars to play in the city that never sleeps? And in the midst of a *pennant race*? Not the perfect plan. The Yankees were finally realistically seeking their first American League or division title in nine years. And they needed to bolster their starting pitching. I was fine with returning to a rotation but in no condition to fulfill their needs for a long period. My promising start in pinstripes did not last long.

11

A SOUR BITE OF
THE BIG APPLE

Gabe Paul had not turned any cartwheels over my behavior and downfall in Cleveland when he was general manager of the Indians. I had done nothing in San Francisco to convince anyone in baseball that my life or career were headed back in the right direction. Yet as spring was about to turn to summer in 1973, I reunited with Paul, who along with Yankees manager Ralph Houk believed I remained viable enough to stick in the rotation during the early stages of a pennant race. Go figure.

I have always suspected that the Giants talked Paul into taking me back with the claim that he had knowingly traded them damaged goods after the 1971 season. I barely spoke with Paul after the deal was consummated between the Giants and Yankees. He told me on the phone that I was getting a chance to start over, gave me some details about meeting the Yankees in Oakland, and that was it. I never said a word after Hello. And I did not talk to him after I arrived because Paul did not hang around the clubhouse. New Yankees owner George Steinbrenner was far more visible to the players. (Steinbrenner had been on the verge of buying the Indians in 1972, and many have speculated whether the club would have remained terrible for another two decades if the deal had gone through.)

The Yankees did not require a sizzling start to embark on a battle for first place in what was an incredibly balanced Eastern Division. They were only a few games over .500 but a half-game out of first place when I arrived. The club made it easy for me. It required just a short trip across the bay from San Francisco to Oakland to join them for a series against the Athletics. And I showed up drunk.

I had flown to Oakland to join the club but remained in my hotel room guzzling for three days rather than going to the ballpark. Among my curious visitors was new teammate Ron Blomberg, who that year earned the distinction as the first designated hitter in baseball history—the American League adopted the designated hitter for that season, and he happened to be the first to come to the plate. Blomberg could scarcely believe his eyes when he entered. My room was littered with liquor bottles and beer cans.

He wrote about that experience in his 2021 book that revolved around his relationship with legendary Yankees catcher Thurman Munson, who was killed in 1979 practicing take offs and landings in a plane he'd bought to fly to his beloved hometown of Canton, Ohio. Blomberg opined that I threw harder than Nolan Ryan, no small feat given that the Express fired fastballs consistently at or above 100 mph.

That is not what Blomberg remembered most about my ill-fated stint in the Big Apple. He related a story in his book about he and Munson spotting me wearing a fluorescent-orange suit and sleeping drunk in a gutter on Boyleston Street at 1:30 a.m. in cold, rainy Boston. He recalled that they dragged me several blocks to the hotel in which the Yankees were staying, but his story is a bit off. What Blomberg did not know was that I had been thrown out of a bar that night for fighting and was so drunk that I failed to give my taxi driver a destination. He pulled over to the side of the road and dumped me out of the cab. That is where Blomberg and Munson found me. And they did not drag me to the hotel. I managed to stumble alongside them as they helped me to my room. Blomberg otherwise had a perfect memory. As he also remembered in his book, I arrived at Fenway Park the next day with two black eyes, courtesy of my combatant the night before.

I can imagine what Blomberg feared his team was getting as the seeds of a pennant race were being planted around the time he visited my room in Oakland. But the Yankees' faith in me appeared justified when I resembled vintage Sam McDowell early in my return to the familiar role of a starting pitcher after serving mostly in the bullpen that year with the Giants. My walks remained concerning and my strikeouts were down but I was missing bats and inducing weak contact. I allowed just 7 earned runs on 23 hits over my first 40 2/3 innings with the Yankees to win 5 of 6 starts. I was still firing my fastball in the 100 mph range. I pitched shutout ball against Chicago and Kansas City in the last of those outings to help catapult the club to the top of the standings.

Then I collapsed—and so did the team. It was not a complete coincidence. I had since joining the Yankees overcome my physical ailments with focus and concentration on the mound. But my worsening alcoholism and the poor self-esteem that had plagued me throughout my life had affected my brain to such as extent that maintaining that level of mental strength proved impossible. One night in Minnesota I was out drinking and tripped on a curb outside a nightclub, resulting in a severely sprained ankle. I lied to Houk about how I sustained the injury then could not pitch for three weeks.

The Yankees would soon have been better off without me the way I performed. I began after my return an epic ten-game losing streak to end the season. I pitched horribly in most starts though it must be cited that the hitting support I received during that stretch reminded me unfavorably of my time in Cleveland. These were not the Yankees of Ruth, Gehrig, DiMaggio, or Mantle. During that horrific period they scored two runs or fewer for me seven times.

I hated New York. I felt lost there. Most players loved it because there was so much to do and the advertising and marketing possibilities seemed endless. Perhaps such opportunities would have been viable during my peak and comparatively sober years but not as I hit thirty years old as a drunken has-been. I took a bite out of the Big Apple and did not like the taste. I was not even trying to adapt. I just yearned to escape.

Only two forms of escape were open to me at the time. One, typically, came with beers in a bar. Another was nostalgia. Yankees pitching coach Whitey Ford would hold court on the bench before games and regale us by reliving his playing days. He would entertain everyone with stories about working with catcher Elston Howard to disfigure baseballs and give them late movement. Ford was not a hard thrower and later in his career he needed to cheat to win. So he had Howard rub the ball against his shin-guard clasps or dip it into a puddle of tobacco juice behind home plate then throw it back to Ford, who fired it to the plate and made it dance.

Ford was not the only engaging storyteller. I would arrive early to hear clubhouse manager Pete Sheehy talk about serving in that same role during the days of Ruth and Gehrig and then DiMaggio. Sheehy recalled being responsible for sobering up the Great Bambino after nights on the town and bringing him to the ballpark when he had fallen asleep in police stations. Nobody dared disturb the great Babe Ruth. The tales told by Sheehy sounded eerily similar to my own escapades—I too required team representatives to release me from the grips of the law after nights of inebriated adventures. In my sick mind at the time I justified my drunkenness by comparing myself to Ruth. Never mind that he could produce and I could not.

Though I had cemented my standing as the worst drunk in baseball as the mid-1970s approached, many ballplayers in that era and beyond could share first-hand stories about overdrinking. Among them was Mickey Mantle, who would show up at spring training and tell tales of his playing career, which ended right before the 1969 season. Among his recollections was his fear of facing me when I was scheduled to pitch for the Indians. He surprised me by revealing his knowledge that I was a big drinker, saying that as a player he'd wondered if I would be tipsy on the mound. Ignorant of the fact that I always performed sober, Mantle had been scared that a drunken Sam with already shaky control who preferred to pitch him high and tight would accidentally fire a fastball at his noggin. The fact is I never knocked down Mantle.

I lived in Manhattan early in my first season with the Yankees. I had no car so I learned to navigate the subway system, which transported me to and from games. I frequented the bars two or three times a week. Upon the arrival of my family we moved to a hotel with a pool in New Jersey, just a short ride across the George Washington Bridge to the stadium.

By 1974 my career was hanging by a thread. I showed up drunk one day in spring training, raising the concern of new Yankees manager Bill Virdon. The club placed me in the hospital for three days to dry out. But I just got wet again. Virdon decided to use me only in relief and as a spot starter. I often that season arrived at the ballpark in an inebriated state.

That did not prevent me from achieving one last hurrah on July 29, 1974, in Boston, a team against which I performed well even as my career was collapsing. My control remained a mess but I was inducing weak contact all night before a big crowd at Fenway Park. I was mowing down a damn good lineup that featured fine hitters such as Carl Yastrzemski, Dwight Evans, and Rick Burleson. The Sox led the American League in runs scored that season but I did not allow a hit until Evans led off the sixth inning with a single. I maintained a 1-0 lead into the eighth when I hung a curve to Evans that he blasted for a home run. After I walked Yastrzemski, I received a visit from Virdon and catcher Thurman Munson, who told his manager that I was still strong and throwing as well as I had in the first inning. Why Virdon even asked Munson about me I will never know—he removed me from the game in favor of super reliever Sparky Lyle, who went on to take a rare defeat.

Munson defended me on that occasion but he had long since grown tired of my act. Even in 1973 I was defiantly ignoring his signs. He insisted to Houk that I be removed because I was not even looking for what he was putting down behind the plate. Houk and Munson yelled at me but I simply continued to throw whatever I wanted. I had lost my motivation to work with my catcher. I had reverted to the old Sam who tried to outguess hitters, which made me care less about the science of pitching and exacerbated my fears.

I had simply stopped caring by then. Playing baseball had become a nuisance, an interruption of my increasingly destructive lifestyle, and my pride as a pitcher had long since dissipated. Among the hassles in 1974 was that the team had moved to Shea Stadium while Yankee Stadium was being renovated. The result was a long trip without a car from my Manhattan hotel to the ballpark. So I moved to a motel across from LaGuardia Airport, from which I took a van to and from games. I spent a disturbing amount of time in the motel bar getting drunk two or three times a week. My drinking binges stopped for a couple of months after my family arrived (though periodically I'd stop at a bar on my way home from the stadium), but when school bells called the kids to return, I was back to getting smashed more often than ever before.

As one might imagine, that was not helping my performance on the mound. I bounced between the bullpen and the rotation like a yo-yo. And how could anyone expect me to schedule my drunks with that setup? My focus and, consequently, my control drifted in and out. My stuff remained viable but neither I nor my opposing hitters could predict where my pitches were headed. I walked seven batters in three innings yet did not allow a run during one wild relief stint against the Red Sox in Fenway Park. The descent from pitcher to thrower that took hold in San Francisco returned in 1974. I was lost and I did not care. The Yankees were more than happy to place me on the disabled list in late May with a slipped disc. There I stayed for two months, which until my family arrived gave me an opportunity to sink further into my depravity.

My lack of control off the field and on the mound remained destructive after I returned late that season. I walked nearly a batter an inning in three starts that resulted in two losses then I completely fell apart. Other pitchers might have felt a strong desire to perform well against a former team but I felt no remorse when the Indians clobbered me twice that year. I finished the season with a 1-6 record, 41 walks in just 49 innings, and a 4.69 ERA.

In reality I did not finish the season at all. I called Paul on September 13 and told him I quit. I decided that I would rather go to the bar and get drunk. The club sent three officials to my hotel to try to convince me to return, though given the way I was pitching and behaving I am not sure why. I defiantly brought out a bottle of Chivas Regal and began drinking it. My guests left and I continued to pour down the scotch until I passed out in mid-afternoon. I remained in the sack for twenty-four hours.

Like George Costanza in an early episode of *Seinfeld*, I returned to work the next day as if nothing had happened. Virdon emerged from his office after a security guard alerted him of my presence in the clubhouse. He sidled up next to me an hour later with word that Paul wanted to meet with me in his trailer office behind the stadium. What followed was meant to be a come-to-Jesus conversation with Paul, who arranged a program during which I would see a psychiatrist once a week in New York then return home to Pittsburgh. What the Yankees did not know was that after seeing the shrink completely sober I would ride the elevator down to the bar and get drunk or head over to LaGuardia to booze it up before flying back to my hometown. That lasted a month. The Yankees had at one point even dispatched their batting practice pitcher to accompany me on road trips to ensure my good behavior. Bad idea. He joined me in a bar in Chicago and got drunk while I stayed sober.

Drinking and drunkenness always progress. Mine did for seventeen years from my first drink to the last but at a pace so subtle that like other alcoholics I could not recognize it and accepted it as normal. I had the added excuse of living a celebrity lifestyle. I could tell myself that Babe Ruth and Mickey Mantle imbibed and they were among the best players in baseball history.

I was full of excuses. I cited infrequent outings and bouncing from starter to reliever to blame my lousy season on Virdon. But looking back one might wonder why he even started me or summoned me from the bullpen in 1974. Aside from my out-of-nowhere gem in Boston, I never performed up to the capabilities of a sober and healthy Sam. I suppose Virdon could not completely ignore anyone wearing the iconic pinstripes, which most donned with reverence but not me. He pretty much did ignore me down the stretch in 1974 and I definitely could not blame him. His team was in a nip-and-tuck battle with Baltimore for the division crown, and I was pitching terribly. As another example of my alcoholic fog, during this time when the Yankees were in a struggle to win the pennant, I had no conscious idea of the struggle or where we were in the standings. I was called upon just once from August 20 forward and that was another poor effort in a loss to Detroit on September 8 that had long been decided by the time I arrived on the mound. My departure from the team came five days later.

I was finished in New York. Yet despite the fact that I hated my experience there and had lost any semblance of intensity for pitching, I reacted defensively and arrogantly after receiving a letter stating I had been released by the team. It was the typical response of an alcoholic. I tried to convince myself it did not matter.

From a practical standpoint, it certainly mattered. About a month went by and I began asking myself what was next for me. Reality had set in. I sensed that the end of my career was coming. I had continued the previous two winters to take courses at Duquesne University and had attended workshops to earn licenses in real estate, insurance, and securities. But the fact remained I could not expect to gain success in any professional endeavor until I sobered up. And

I was not ready for that. I was lucky that I continued to get paid by the Yankees until my contract officially ran out on December 31.

The uncertainty of my future caused sleepless nights. I decided to continue my playing career—if any team would take me. The most logical choice was my hometown Pirates. I set up a meeting with general manager Joe Brown, who wasted no time in asking about what he termed "my drinking problem" and added that he preferred not to deal with it. To claim I never had trouble stopping after a beer or two at that point in my career would have been ludicrous. I acknowledged the problem but defended my current status by lying. I claimed I had addressed the issue by working with a priest and was no longer partaking. He told me he would think about it. It had become obvious to me that every team in baseball knew I was a drunk. The question whether any team would take a chance on me was answered when I worked out a deal with the Pirates.

It was not exactly an arrangement that had me jumping for joy. Only if I promised not to drink and performed well enough to land a job in spring training would I be offered a contract. So what did this alcoholic do? He got drunk on the way to camp and created a scene at the motel in Bradenton upon his arrival. I could have easily been dispatched from the club before I threw my first pitch but I pulled an explanation out of my butt, telling Brown that our agreement stated I could not drink during spring training, which had yet to begin, and I was merely celebrating my last day of drinking. I supposed he believed I had him on a technicality, so he accepted my bullshit and allowed me to continue.

There were no other open doors. I performed or I was out of baseball. What would win—my addiction or my dedication? For a while it was the latter. I worked my ass off and focused well enough to outpitch the competition. And just before the final cutdown the Pirates signed me to a contract for the 1975 season. I was upset at being relegated to a bullpen role with the likelihood of an occasional spot start but even that was a tall order given the talent and depth on the Pittsburgh staff that included veterans such as Bruce Kison, Jerry Reuss, Dock Ellis, and Jim Rooker as well as talented rookie and eventual twenty-game-winner John Candelaria.

I was in no position to complain. That I felt I deserved to knock any of them out of the rotation was the basic arrogance of an alcoholic. I should have felt fortunate just to be wearing the uniform of my hometown team and receiving an opportunity to pitch for a club that boasted one of the premier lineups in the sport. Stars such as Manny Sanguillen, Willie Stargell, Richie Zisk, Al Oliver, and Dave Parker could transform any mediocre outing for a hurler into a victory.

But I certainly performed better in Pittsburgh than I had at any time since I left Cleveland. Early in my stint with the Pirates I nearly eliminated my drinking. That helped me focus on the mound. Another major factor was that my role as a long reliever and spot starter provided more time for my shoulder to heal between appearances. The same was true when I received extra days off after outings with San Francisco.

All remained fine until our first road trip to Los Angeles in mid-May. I had a friend there with whom I would traditionally down some alcohol after every game. We arrived early in the afternoon on an off day. I was feeling a little sick but I was not about to skip an opportunity to drink. My buddy Bob picked me up and we began boozing. I got so smashed that he needed to carry me back to my hotel room. He tucked me in around 10 p.m., and twice during the early morning I vomited. At noon I was sweating profusely. I called my friend, returned to bed, then awoke for another round of barfing. By that time I was supposed to be on the team bus headed for the stadium.

I called Bob begging him to find a doctor—any doctor—who would make a special trip to the hotel to take care of me. Bob also sent a note to Pirates manager Danny Murtaugh explaining I was very sick and would not be there for the game. The doctor arrived around 9 p.m. and determined that my temperature had reached 103. He provided some antibiotics and instructed me to drink plenty of liquids and soups. I went back to sleep and awoke at eight the next morning. Bob even delivered the doctor's note to Murtaugh.

I stayed in bed until the next day. Soon Brown paid me a visit. He told me to shower and accompany the team to San Francisco for a series against my old teammates. I remained so weak I could barely stand up when I was called into a lost-cause second game, yet I worked my way out of jams to pitch shutout ball.

All remained well from a pitching standpoint. I even won a spot start against the eventual world champion Cincinnati Reds. But I could not stop drinking on the road. Living with my family presented me with few opportunities during home stands so I really cut loose away from Pittsburgh. Soon thereafter we visited New York for a series against the Mets, where I performed as I did during my peak with four shutout innings and four strikeouts. I then embarked on a celebration that marked the beginning of the end of my career. I got so hammered at a club that I was still feeling the effects in the locker room the next day. I was so unsteady warming up that day that my pitches landed in another zip code. Bullpen catcher Don Leppert took me by the arm to keep me from falling and escorted me to the clubhouse whirlpool where an hour-long soak helped me sweat it out. I then sat on the bus and waited for the players to arrive. They said nothing to me but management certainly took notice. The Pirates were in first place with a deep and talented pitching staff. They did not need a drunk among them no matter how well he was pitching.

Soon we were flying to Philadelphia. Our pitching coach called upon me for an eighty-minute running session in the outfield. I was next summoned into the second game of a doubleheader and again pitched well. I allowed just one run in four innings. Little did I know that would be my swan song in major league baseball. I had yet to be reprimanded for my hangover in New York so I thought perhaps I had dodged a bullet.

No such luck. Brown tapped me on the shoulder during our flight home the next day and said he wanted to see me early the following morning in his office. The jig was up. The meeting lasted about three minutes. "Sam, you know what this is all about," he said. I did. I had been released.

News travels fast. That afternoon I received a call from old Cleveland teammate Dick Howser, who was now managing the Kansas City Royals. He offered to sign me for the same salary but start me out at Triple-A. He received a typically arrogant response from an alcoholic: Thanks but no thanks. He was a friend, so I confided in him. I told him I was through with baseball and that I enjoyed playing but not "the other." What was the other? I did not know. All I knew was that I could not understand or control what was going on in my life.

I would eventually learn, but not before I suffered a breakdown so severe and traumatic that I nearly did not survive.

Sam's 1960 high school
senior-year photo

The McDowell siblings in 2001
(Sam upper right)

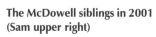

Publicity photo with the great Sandy Koufax during spring training, 1964

Publicity photo with future teammate Dean Chance in spring training, 1965

Sam collecting his thoughts before a start in 1965

Indians catcher Del Crandall and Sam in a meeting of the minds on the mound, 1966

CLEVELAND INDIANS 1966 YEARBOOK

Fireballing Sam on the cover of the 1966 Indians yearbook

Sam signing autographs for Indians fans in Cleveland, 1968

Sam (second from right) with (from left) Steve Hargan, Sonny Siebert, and Luis Tiant, one of the finest rotations in baseball history, 1968

Sam in action on the mound, 1970

Family Day at Municipal Stadium with first wife Carol Ann and kids Debbie and Tim

Sam about to unleash a pitch for the Indians, 1971

Sam in his first year with the San Francisco Giants, 1972

Family Day with the Yankees in 1973 alongside son Tim

Looking thoughtful in pinstripes, 1974

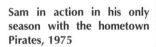

Sam in action in his only
season with the hometown
Pirates, 1975

Matching Pirates uniforms: Sam in 1975 and son Tim in 1988

Sam speaking at a drug and alcohol convention, 2001

Sam playing golf with former NFL players, 2002

Taking it easy on his Clermont golf course, 2002

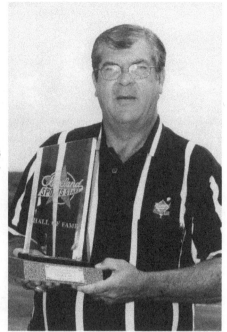

Sam receiving an award for his efforts in creating a drug-free-school program in Florida, 2004

Modern-day Sam and his smile of contentment

THE LOST YEARS

It was 1979. I was driving early in the morning in a condition sometimes expressed euphemistically as "feeling no pain." (How I survived all my drunk driving at that time in my life is beyond me.) I swerved and hit the tire of a semi truck. That threw me into the next lane of traffic and through a guardrail on the Highland Park Bridge, which rested 129 feet above the largest river in Pittsburgh and about 100 yards from one of its most powerful dams. Had I hit the water or the riverbank, I would have been dead.

Earlier that day a tree company had dumped two truckloads of tree chips on the riverbank. As fate or God would have it, I landed upside down on that pile of wood chips, sustaining only a broken collarbone and two ribs. As I lay in the hospital, my mother grew philosophical and uttered words that would haunt me for quite a while: "God has something in mind for you. If not your life would be over." I thought about that remark throughout my three days there.

Not that it stopped me from drinking. My son Tim, to whom I have grown so close since my recovery allowed him to love a healthy father, quoted the first passage from the Charles Dickens classic *A Tale of Two Cities* to capture his childhood thoughts and feelings about our relationship.

> It was the best of times, it was the worst of times, it was the age of wisdom, it was the age of foolishness, it was the epoch of belief, it was the epoch of incredulity, it was the season of Light, it was the season of Darkness, it was the spring of hope, it was the winter of despair, we had everything before us, we had nothing before us.

Carol Ann once told him that he could love his dad and hate the alcoholic— quite profound and astute for a woman who never took a counseling class. She had no inkling of the deep impact her words would make on her son. Tim once told me that those words, uttered when he was twelve years old, lifted the dark clouds from his psyche and replaced them with sunshine. They enabled him to embrace the love he felt for me but acknowledge the anger he experienced when I went off on one of my many binges before and after I retired from baseball. They did not lessen the terrible effect my alcoholism had on my family, but they helped Tim maintain his sanity through it all.

Tim and I talk often about the bad old days when he and his sister Debbie would walk by me in the driveway as they left for school and see that I had again passed out after another night of binge boozing. He spoke about his contradictory emotions—feeling both secure and fearful about his and his family's future. He told me of his pervasive sense of unpredictability, not knowing when he would see his dad and in what condition I would be in.

It was indeed the best and worst of times for Tim. During my playing days he would spend time with me in clubhouses and experience the thrill of shaking hands with real major league stars. He would join me in spring training during breaks from school; spend summers in the cities in which I played, including San Francisco and New York; attend All-Star Games, celebrity events, and banquets; frequent exclusive resorts. How many children of alcoholics can make such a claim?

But there were the ugly memories as well. Some have faded over time, but others never will. He remembers me being out of his life after I had engaged in benders that lasted several days and often ended in a car accident or early-morning trip to the hospital or someone returning me to our doorstep a stumbling mess. And there were the promises. "Dad is going to get help," I would tell him. "Dad is serious this time. He is going to get sober." Tim told me once he remembered thinking that he could never again feel comfortable trusting that I would ever dry out.

That was something he yearned for so desperately. He wanted to be proud of his father. He stuffed shoe boxes with photos of me in action on the mound to show his classmates. He told them about my blurry-fast fastball. He told them I had played in six All-Star Games. He told them I was on the cover of *Sports Illustrated*. Little could he have imagined those would be the least of my accomplishments. He would eventually be far prouder of me for my recovery and forty years of sobriety, the 3 a.m. calls from panicked athletes that I never let ring their way to voicemail, the hours I spent talking to an alcoholic or drug addict as well as their children or spouses. He is honored to be the son of a man who has saved hundreds of athletes and family members. And that makes me happy. True happiness? I never experienced it until I achieved sobriety.

I sure did not experience it immediately following my retirement from base-ball. The fog in which I walked had around my entire life became thicker and darker. I lost all control. I never knew when I would get drunk or to what level. Quite often I tell myself, "Not tonight! I am not going into a bar!" Then I'd find myself in a bar, where I would say in my mind, "Okay, only two drinks tonight." A couple hours later I'd be smashed.

A friend of the family who owned a real estate company set me up with my first job out of baseball. I hated it. I had been used to action on the field. Now I was sitting around all day waiting for the phone to ring. That was the only way to get customers, who were not exactly ringing that phone off the hook. I was paid only on commission so the work was not swelling the old bank account. It was fortunate I was still receiving paychecks from the Pirates through 1975 because I sold just one home.

I then quit to take another job that also paid by commission, this one hawk-ing policies for Colonial Life & Accident Insurance Company in Pittsburgh. I performed better in that position and even set sales records. But my boss was well aware of my drinking problem—it was not hard to figure out why I went AWOL for periods of time. His threats to fire me were hollow because I was his top salesperson. But I eventually descended to the point at which I was no good to anyone—employer or family member.

What I sought from alcohol I could never truly achieve. A person with an addiction seeks peace and happiness through a chemical. He yearns to be funny, to enjoy life, to fit in, to belong. In other words, to be a normal human being. Because of my chronic depression, loneliness, and low self-esteem, these desires were ever-present. They did not subside. Changes take place within addicts when the alcohol or drug hits the blood stream. I was trying to find contentment in a bottle more often than ever before.

The effect on my life proved catastrophic but I remained unwilling or at least unready to even try to kick the habit. I agreed at the insistence of my boss to see a psychiatrist. He sent me to Dr. Abraham Twerski, who I believe to be the fore-most authority on addiction in the world. I should have embraced the chance to work with such an expert who happened to work out of the Pittsburgh area and who had founded the Gateway Rehabilitation Center. But I was not apprecia-tive of the opportunity. I spoke with him for nearly an hour with an arrogant and stubborn mindset as he talked knowledgeably about alcoholism. The old chestnut about having to admit you have a problem before you can really get help came into play and I dismissed Twerski out of hand, telling him he had no idea what he was talking about. I left the room but not before he uttered the words that would stay with me until I got clean: "I'll see you again and hopefully your brain will still be intact." He did and it was—barely. My life spiraled out of control after I met with Twerski.

By that time my drinking binges had increased to four or five times a week. And they were not short inebriations during which I would have a few drinks, go home to sleep it off, and be fine the next day. Quite often I embarked on bouts of boozing that had me snockered for days at a time. My drunkenness peaked from 1976 to 1980. I got arrested seven times during that period for public intoxication, drunk driving, or disturbing the peace. But I was never convicted. The cops would allow me to sit in the chief's office for several hours or sleep it off in a cell. In the meantime I was trying to sell insurance, and my finances were becoming strapped. So I sold the dream home into which we had recently moved and we hightailed it to the country, about ten miles from Monroeville. It was what those in the field of addiction refer to as a "geographical cure"—basically an escape in the illogical hope that a clean slate might help. I had severe worries about my drinking but could no longer control it as I did to some extent during my baseball career.

Most of the bars in my hometown of Monroeville had banned me permanently. The establishments were intended to be havens for folks who wished to drink or grab a bite peacefully and not saloons frequented by angry, violent drunks either crying in their beer or starting brawls. We had only lived in our new home for about eighteen months when my wife and family bolted from me permanently. Now I was close to bars that did not know enough about my escapades to ban me. But those I visited after our move soon also told me to get lost and never come back. Some of them I never would have frequented during my baseball career. They were strictly skid row joints.

When Carol left me again, this time for good, and moved into a Monroeville apartment. I was in no position or state of mind to fight for anything so I gave her all our furniture. My eighteen-year marriage soon collapsed, and she received full custody of Debbie and Tim. I was scared to death. I continued to convince myself that alcoholism was not the problem. But my sense of fear and loneliness had been exacerbated. How was I going to take charge of my life?

I had certainly taken charge of a bottle. Among my drinking binges was a ten-day marathon that I somehow survived. My bouts often took place during the frigid Pittsburgh winters. I would pass out in my car, sometimes in below-zero temperatures. At one point Tim came to visit to see how I was doing. Carol had driven him as he was adamant about wanting to see me and she waited in the car. He saw ten bottles of booze on the floor of my bedroom and me only semi-sober before taking off.

My family had finally been pushed to the edge. So had my finances. I sold my house and moved into my parents' home in Highland Park in February 1980. I had child support and alimony payments to make, and I was earning very little money. I had resumed selling insurance but remained on commission only. I felt a strong sense of embarrassment and shame returning to live with my folks, but I had no alternative. My mother issued the same edict as had the Pirates five years earlier: drink and you are gone. But I was not a child. There were no babysitters for thirty-six-year-old men. My folks could not keep an eye on me 24/7. When my mom left for six days in April to visit my sister two months after my arrival, I promptly got drunk. I came home and was passed out on the kitchen floor after my mother came back. My brother woke me up and dragged me to my bed.

The time of reckoning was near. I rose at 3 a.m. and prepared a pot of coffee. I paced the living room floor for hours. All I remember of that dark moment was repeating both to myself and to my demon addiction, "You beat me, you beat me, you beat me." I feared that I was going insane—I was thinking real insanity.

The final crossroad had been reached. Did I want to live or die? I wanted to live. But did I want to live desperately enough to act? There was little clarity in my thinking, but I did know that I was surely digging an early grave if I did not gain sobriety. So at 10 a.m. I called the operator and asked her to connect me with Gateway. I did not remember the rest of the business name—thank goodness I recalled that much of it. She could have sent me to Gateway anything since there were more than fifteen different businesses or schools with that name but she hooked me up with the right one. I assume she received many calls asking for that number.

I could no longer reject the warnings of Dr. Twerski. He would indeed see me again, and my brain was indeed still intact, though quite damaged. My brother drove me the forty-five minutes from Highland Park to Gateway in Aliquippa. He barely spoke en route. I was deathly afraid that my condition would earn me institutionalization for life. This is no exaggeration. I had stumbled into a barrier I could not break through, an issue I could not resolve. I had always found ways to extricate myself out of jams. But not this time. Addiction had beaten me though I had yet to recognize that as my primary demon. I feared that nothing I could do would help. I believed it to be a mental illness or character flaw.

When I arrived Twerski was the first to greet me. He had been waiting for me in front of the elevator doors with open arms. We were about to engage in an all-out battle to pull me out of my personal Hell.

13

GATEWAY TO SOBRIETY

Those who do not understand the alcoholic personality might be flabbergasted to learn that I was unaware of my addiction when I arrived at the Gateway Rehabilitation Center in 1980. After all, how could anyone who embarked on a ten-day drinking binge, passed out in his car overnight in freezing temperatures, and had lost his wife and kids not know he was an alcoholic?

But it was true. I knew something was seriously wrong with me, which is why I checked into the facility. My assumption, however, was that I was insane. Addiction is never obvious to the addicted. That is why addiction is known in the field of medicine as the most treacherous of all diseases because the body and mind demand the chemical, eventually refusing all of our normal survival instincts toward shelter, food, sex. There had been a chemical imbalance within me from birth that automatically altered my frontal lobe, thereby numbing or desensitizing the area of the brain affecting such thought processes and emotions as critical thinking, fear, logic, and judgment. And because of all the chemical changes and differences in the addicted person, once he or she takes a mind-altering substance such as alcohol or a drug, that substance becomes paramount in that person's hierarchy of the above survival instincts.

I indeed believed I was insane. I wrongly assumed that if I weren't insane I would be capable of controlling my intake. I felt that I had proven my exceptional willpower throughout my amateur and professional baseball career and that I could win any battle with determination alone. I had also extensively studied basic and abnormal psychology through books and tapes during my playing days. I ignorantly related what I was experiencing to many of the disorders

I learned about. Therefore, I must be crazy. And I embraced that belief with deadly seriousness.

The first week of my twenty-eight–day, in-patient stay proved uneventful and unexciting. It was designed to ensure that I was stable physically and mentally and that detoxification was not necessary. Cutting off alcohol can prove dangerous and life threatening to some alcoholics. It can result in shock and even death. I soon underwent a complete psychosocial interview to provide the Gateway therapists with a synopsis of my emotional and psychological health. The therapists' initial concerns are depression and the possibility of suicide. I was interviewed during a counseling session to determine if other problems existed within me, such as mental illness or other disorders. But addiction is a primary disease, which means no matter what other issues are present, including mental illness, the alcoholism requires the initial focus and treatment. If the addiction is not addressed first, there can be no help, cure, and resolution.

Since I was deemed stable, the therapy and educational aspects of my treatment began during my second week at Gateway. I underwent one-on-one counseling with a licensed therapist three days a week. That transformed my addictogenic personality and mindset to a normal, healthy one that would lead me to exhibiting more appropriate behavior. During that same period in rehab, I attended seminars that taught patients like me all about addiction, including how we contracted it. The sessions taught us that the disease is genetic. It showed us the chemical changes in the brain and the resulting abnormal workings of the pain and pleasure centers as well as the altered state of the decision making part of the mind, which is in the frontal lobe.

What an incredible learning experience! The relevance to every one of us as we sat in that room was palpable. Those who took the sessions seriously (there were some who had been legally forced to attend, had no intention of changing, and so did not) understood what was being explained to them. I could see it in their body movements, their simple head shakes. I strongly sensed that those who did not physically react allowed the teachings to stream in one ear and out the other. But most of the patients soaked it in and took it sincerely. After the talks, when we were all alone, we discussed what we had just heard.

Soon came the greatest epiphany of my life. I had assumed upon my arrival at Gateway that I suffered from a mental illness because I had tried everything to stop drinking and had failed, though such a claim could certainly be refuted. After two weeks of rehab, I realized I had a bona fide disease. That mistaken identity was greatly a product of the times. Addiction for centuries and well into the 1970s had been considered a character flaw, a mental illness, a psychological defect. Physical research data thought to prove otherwise was uncovered late that decade by a researcher who studied cancer tumors and found tetrahydroisoquinoline (THIQ) in the brains of alcoholics but not normal people. At the time, researchers believed THIQ might be implicated in alcoholism, but this theory is no longer accepted.

Even so, since that researcher's discovery, new research has confirmed that addiction is a disease. One study at the Carnegie Mellon Research Center in 2005 showed that in alcoholics and other drug addicts, the frontal lobe, which controls our fear, logic, and sense of reality and decision making, is anesthetized. It also demonstrated that the frontal lobe regenerates after sixteen to eighteen weeks of proper recovery from addiction. Doctors have marveled in recent years at what they see in their patients after recovery. This is no longer a theory. It is a proven fact based on nearly a half-century of research and to which I can personally attest.

I was truthful about my thoughts, feelings, and life story from the start at Gateway. But I was quiet and noncommittal. I felt skeptical that the struggles and commitments laid in front of me could solve my problems. The ignorance of my belief system had been so cemented over the years that I could not see any light at the end of the tunnel. But I opened up quickly. I could see that all of us were in the same boat. We were all drunks or drug addicts with similar behavioral issues.

Twerski came to the rescue willingly and passionately. My amazement at his story and admiration for his work continued to grow with time and exposure. He was an orthodox Jewish rabbi who had graduated from the Marquette University medical school in 1960, trained in psychiatrics at the University of Pittsburgh, and later headed the Department of Psychiatry at St. Francis Hospital, specializing in alcoholism and addiction. He combined his Rabbinical teachings on morality and ethics with his education in psychiatry before opening Gateway, which has helped thousands of people gain new leases on life. Twerski was a strong believer in the Twelve Steps program embraced by Alcoholics Anonymous (AA). I embarked on it after my stay at Gateway. It allowed me to remain on the path to mental, emotional, and physical health.

Other therapists worked the day-to-day therapy and counseling during my time at Gateway while Twerski served as the medical director who provided physical examinations and ran most of the educational seminars. We watched films about addiction and received a tremendous amount of educational material, including one book simply titled *The Big Book*, which is the bible of AA and a pathway to success for those in recovery.

Carol and the kids were invited to the facility to confront me with their thoughts and feelings. That was quite an eye-opener. It proved very emotional for me because I had been so wrapped up in my own life that I had been deaf and blind to how my addiction was affecting them as well as my parents. My mother called my therapist unbeknownst to me and asked for advice regarding my return. Should we hide the booze in our house? The answer was no. Should we talk avoid talking about our son's alcoholism? No, talk about it often. Should we make sure he attends his AA meetings? No. If he goes, he goes. But *show faith in your son*.

Toward the end of my time at Gateway, all the misconceptions I had about my drinking problem had been educated out of my mind. But my recovery had barely begun. The potential of falling back into bad habits was frighteningly real to all of us who left the premises. The seminars in our final days at the center focused on our new, sensitive, realistic, healthy psyche and how to maintain it. It was all new to us as recovering addicts. We were told never to get too hungry or lonely or tired or angry. Those were cues that could launch a relapse process. They might start a chain reaction and trigger a setback into old and dangerous behavior. We were warned that the old addictogenic thinking within our subconscious would remain for quite some time. It would yearn for that old feeling and would give us an excuse to start drinking or doing drugs again.

I had to be aware of my thirty years of thinking a certain way. Now all of that had changed. We had been therapeutically taught a new way of reasoning and acting. The goal was to continue that path so we could ultimately change into realistic, honest, logical, decent human beings.

Gateway was a test. But it was not the ultimate test. Gateway was a controlled environment. My honesty with Twerski and the therapists, my willingness to soak in all I learned, and my desire to rid myself of a debilitating disease were positive steps. Yet they would mean nothing if I could not apply my new knowledge practically. My understanding that alcoholism was a treatable disease rather than a reflection of my weaknesses gave me hope and strength. Now I needed to continue the path to sobriety and wellness.

Though it takes up to four months for a recovering addict to recognize a magnificent change in themselves that might be perceived as a miracle, my loved ones noticed a nearly immediate difference. Before leaving Gateway on May 1, I was taught what to expect internally after six weeks and beyond if I embraced the Twelve Steps program.

Among those who required far less time to recognize a positive trend was Tim. I have spoken often with him about his observations at the time. He detected that I began living my life so differently that he felt in his heart that I was destined for a permanent and wonderful change. He observed my mindfulness about everything I did, particularly my attending AA meetings as if my life depended on it, which I believed it did. Tim told me that he was unaware that I felt my very existence hinged on strict adherence.

He also remarked that he began to see me as the humblest human being he had ever known—quite a departure from my pre-Gateway reality. I had before my recovery been quite opinionated. If I did not know something I would always hazard a guess so as not to be perceived as ignorant. I have to smile when he recalls the first time during my recovery he asked me something about addiction. I replied, "I don't know . . . let me check with my sponsor."

Tim has also reminded me of an incident when I was running late to an AA meeting, parked illegally, and got a ticket. He asked me if I was planning on getting one of my police friends to fix it. After all, even though it was years after my retirement from baseball, I was still a big name in Pittsburgh. But I replied to my son, "No, I screwed up. I need to pay this fine." When Tim relived this story, he expressed a sense of wonderment about his changing father. "I didn't know this new guy but I loved what I was seeing and couldn't wait to see what was next."

He believed what was next was continued sobriety. Tim was quite aware that I had gone five or six months without drinking at times previously and that only a month had passed since I had graduated from Gateway. But his "Dad radar" was telling him that this time something was different. He said he would have bet his life that I had taken my last drink. He was right. The effort I put into my recovery and the drastic changes I was making in my life were beginning to tear down the protective wall he had built between us. It allowed him to promote within himself a sense of hope and belief that I would remain sober.

My stay at Gateway and resulting optimism about my future as Sober Sam freed my mind to consider potential options in my personal and professional life. Among them was reconciliation with Carol. I had before my rehab visited her and my then-teenage children at her apartment. I mentioned the possibility of getting back together but she had grown beyond skeptical of my promises, which I had always broken. She replied that if I got help and proved myself with one year of sobriety, she would think about reuniting. Nobody knew at the time I was heading to Gateway—that was a spur-of-the-moment decision made after my breakdown at my parents' house.

After my month-long treatment I visited the kids often but nothing was said between Carol and me about our future together though I learned she was dating other men. I dropped the idea in part because as a more clear-headed and thoughtful person, I felt she deserved some peace and happiness for a change and I did not feel it would be right to interrupt the new lifestyle she had adopted. Soon she was living with another guy and I had begun dating as well though not so often as I had my schedule quite full meeting AA obligations, selling insurance, undergoing special counseling with Twerski, and working with neighborhood children. The latter endeavor would prove particularly rewarding. I assumed for a couple of years after leaving Gateway that it would be my next career.

Another curve that life might have thrown at me was a return to baseball. I did some serious reflecting on the viability of a comeback. I was only thirty-seven and, heck, some pitchers thrive into their mid-forties. My arm was certainly fresh after five years away from the sport. I competed in an old-timers game in Jacksonville, and not just for fun. While warming up I tried to capture my previous form. I lobbed throws during the game for hitters to blast out of the park, as is expected in such an exhibition, but I was not the only person in attendance thinking about a comeback. Another was a scout waiting for a Triple-A game to start who clocked my fastball in the upper-90s during the warm-up session. He asked me if I would be interested in returning to the game. Given the million-dollar contracts that were being tossed about with the advent of free agency, a new phenomenon in major league baseball from which I could have benefitted if I had stayed on the straight and narrow, it was a proposal I had to consider. I mulled it over and even discussed it with Twerski.

I ultimately decided that my sobriety was too important to be jeopardized by a return to baseball. My priorities had changed dramatically. They had shifted from what the so-called celebrity lifestyle offered me, which led to dishonesty, self-loathing, and guilt, to what recovery had provided. And that was honesty, pride, and self-respect. Perhaps I could have revived my baseball career successfully. But I simply could not take the chance.

Maybe a return would have been possible had I established a permanent sobriety. It was still too early in the game in 1980. My focus remained entirely on maintaining sobriety and becoming a good man, living a productive life, helping others. My name was still Sam McDowell. But those who knew the old Sam could hardly recognize the new one. They liked what they saw. And so did I when I looked in the mirror.

14

MY NEW LIFE

The narcissistic, self-centered Sam who walked the earth seeking approval and an escape from reality had been replaced at the Gateway Rehabilitation Center. It was as if the Wizard of Oz had given me a heart. My self-image and pride were now driven not by bolstering my ego but rather by helping others. Among my first ventures after I had established sobriety in the early 1980s was coaching youth baseball.

My original intent was to help my son Tim and his team on the field. But eventually I began to focus beyond teaching the kids of Monroeville to throw strikes, hit a curveball, or field a grounder. I took my responsibilities outside athletic pursuits quite seriously. I deemed it an honor to be a mentor and friend as well as a coach. The kids used me as a sounding board who could provide sage advice about a variety of personal problems. I was sometimes summoned by a teenager past midnight to talk about drug abuse, alcoholism, or issues with family members. I never told them to wait for the morning. We would sit and talk on a curb because no restaurant was open that late. I would listen intently but did not feel comfortable early in my relationships with youth dispensing advice. Among the troubled that sought out my counsel, two became doctors and a third a child psychologist. Others blossomed into successful business-people. I still feel a sense of satisfaction from helping them along life's way.

By the time an athlete is seven to ten years old and has proven to be greatly superior to others their age, they are told incessantly about their God-given talent. I certainly was. Such proclamations remove the satisfaction and pride they receive from the hard work they have put into their sport. That can cause psychological scars that kids that age are too young to grasp. They do not even realize they were working hard to perfect their craft. They were just trying to have fun playing the sport.

The cheapening of achievements weakens self-esteem among children and teenagers. And that is a precursor to depression. When a kid is told a million times that he has natural ability, it begins to sink in. Most individuals gain self-esteem and confidence through accomplishments, overcoming adversity, and realizing they have done so. But not that "special" ballplayer. He is told that he was born to be great.

Most of the youngsters who confided in me did not fall into that category. They were plagued by a myriad of personal problems. It did take me some time to embrace the challenge of working with teenagers. I must admit my initial reluctance and fear. I felt unqualified at first to respond so I sent them to Twerski. I expressed to him my concern that I would say something wrong and send a child in a wrong direction. He laughed and said, "Sam, you're not that powerful" and eventually told me straight out, "You help them." He had more confidence in me than I had in myself but that gave me faith and courage. Twerski reminded me that I could not change anybody who was unwilling to change themselves. He dispatched me to the library to read books on counseling. Fateful journeys indeed.

My early counseling sessions with kids that sometimes lasted past midnight were among the most rewarding experiences of my life, more so than anything I had ever achieved on the mound. That period following my four-week stay at Gateway proved incredibly vibrant and enriching. The fog in which I had been walking around since I could remember had been lifted. It had been replaced by a clear head and the positivity that comes with possibilities. There was no more brooding, no more lying around, no more drinking. I would be in bed around midnight, up by 6:30, and out the door two hours later.

I was selling insurance by day then attending seminars Twerski recommended and going to AA meetings every night I was not scheduled to be elsewhere. I had been asked upon my departure from Gateway to attend ninety AA sessions in ninety days. I informed my therapist that such a commitment was impossible as I was coaching my son's baseball team twice a week. He did not argue as he did with others who claimed they could not join in because he believed in my sincerity. After the baseball season I indeed went to ninety meetings in ninety days and remained faithful in my obligations.

I found it interesting, as I researched the history of AA, to learn that it was founded by a salesman and doctor, both of whom were alcoholics. Their first meeting was in Akron, Ohio, but their second was held right in my hometown of Pittsburgh. That was my AA home group. Each patient has his or her own but we were able to visit each other's home group. I did just that while never failing to attend my own sessions. I felt a sense of dedication and purpose previously foreign to me.

My experience at Gateway proved fruitful beyond embracing the pathway to sobriety. I made new friends among the patients. We helped each other stay on the right road. Some among the eighty-five in our graduating class were not dedicated to recovery and failed to take their post-stay steps seriously, but I enjoyed the company of and my camaraderie with those who did. We would meet for coffee and pizza after many of the AA meetings. Some questioned what they had been taught at Gateway and some of the Twelve Steps but most seemed dedicated to ridding themselves of their addictions.

I was saddened to notice, however, that our AA group meetings were becoming more sparsely attended, then I learned that many had relapsed into their addiction. Six months after I left Gateway, I discovered that I was the only patient from my graduating class who had remained in recovery and sober. There were happy endings, however. Some returned to the meetings and gained success after their first or second or third or even fourth relapse. Within a couple of years, about twenty in our class remained in recovery. Their failures and successes proved to be a wonderful learning experience for me. I gained tremendous knowledge about how they treated their educational programs, therapy sessions, and Twelve Steps program and why they fell back into their bad habits.

My yearning to thrive was intense. I wanted sobriety in the worst way after learning that alcoholism was a disease rather than a mental illness. I also sought to share the secrets of my success with others so they could learn from them. Twerski thought the same way. So eight months after graduation he elicited my help with a group he called the Winners Circle, which consisted of patients who had experienced multiple relapses and met at St. Francis Hospital.

That facility was the only detox center in the Pittsburgh area. The recovering addicts, dressed in hospital garb consisting of pajamas and bathrobe, were herded to the thirteenth-floor porch—so much for superstition. Those with three or more years of continuous sobriety hosted the meetings. Each patient was asked, "Why are you here?" If any falsehoods or excuses were uttered, the veterans would shout out, "Bullshit, bullshit, bullshit!" Eventually by way of these confrontations, the patients would admit to where they failed to follow the suggested recovery program (though because of the confrontations these could not be considered AA meetings). I found the sessions fascinating.

Sliding away is much easier than sticking with it. That is one reason relapses are so common. The story of one long-time patient named Ace scared me then and still does to this day because it proved how fragile the process and those in it can be. He had been twenty-one years sober. He attended AA meetings devotedly. He worked in a steel mill and did so faithfully, riding to work and back home on streetcars and buses since he had no transportation of his own. So here he came in his jammies and robe to admit that after two decades he had gotten lazy. He figured he could slip a bit and skip a few meetings. Eventually he would miss more sessions. Ace soon fell back into bad drinking habits and drunkenness. Two weeks after leaving St. Francis, after failing again to follow the recovery program and with the return of addiction depression, Ace committed suicide.

There but for the grace of God go I. His story bolstered my determination to never let my guard down. I met with Twerski an average of once a week for about four years in the early- to mid-1980s. Sometimes we talked three or four times in a week, other times I was absent for nearly a month. It all depended on my schedule or if I required help with an explanation or understanding a book I was reading, workshop I was attending, or tape I was listening to. I had become a voracious learner about addiction and its treatment. He eventually asked me to accompany or follow him to speaking sessions in Ohio, Pennsylvania, and West Virginia. Twerski understood I had an old "drunk mobile" and little money to spend on gasoline so I could not afford to travel any real distances. He suggested I attend some workshops around the tri-state area on addiction. At this point I couldn't afford the fees but eventually and over the next two decades I attended over forty workshops.

I cannot overstate the value of my education in forging a post-baseball career. Certainly much of the credit belongs to the man I could see in the mirror and be proud of by the early 1980s. But my turnaround in life would never have been possible without the tough love and expertise I received from Twerski. He not only spurred my recovery but directed me into a new and rewarding profession as a counselor who helps athletes often hindered on the field and suffering off it from the same disease that had plagued me for nearly two decades. The good doctor believed not only that others in the same boat would respect my background as a ballplayer but that I boasted the potential as a person to advise those in trouble.

I remained skeptical for years that I could be as effective as those with far more experience educationally and professionally. But sometimes I stumbled upon so-called experts who had no idea what they were talking about, and that allowed me to understand my worth. I recall listening to a doctor on a national news network one morning claiming that alcoholism and drug addiction were not diseases. This blew my mind because the physician was considered among the foremost probiotic surgeons in the country and had even launched a robotic operating room in the Dominican Republic. Granted he was not an addiction specialist, but he certainly should have known better. The utterance of views like his is one reason there remains a tragic amount of ignorance in the United States on the subject.

The doctor I heard on TV is not the only medical professional I've encountered who failed to understand addiction. This should come as no surprise considering the little education they receive on the subject. Twerski would continually cite, despite the length of time spent in medical school, how little of it centered on alcoholism and drug abuse. Perhaps they were shown an hour-long film on the subject before moving on. From all I have learned, I can state categorically this to be the case. But a vast amount of research has since proven enlightening to doctors. It has become public knowledge that addiction is indeed as much a disease as cancer and hepatitis. Most doctors who gain this knowledge have learned from the research of others. But what is most important is that they now understand the truth. Well, at least most of them do.

They would have known much earlier had they worked with Twerski. I would have as well. His strong suggestions that I embrace coursework on and reading about addiction not only aided me in my recovery but planted the seed in my heart that I yearned to aid the afflicted and in my mind that I could do so successfully. I knew that my personal experiences as a ballplayer and addict gave me a perspective that other athletes would respect. But that was merely a bonus. My knowledge base and ability to make a difference required intensive study and a passionate desire to help others.

After all, lives and careers were at stake. This was not about helping a pitcher get a sharper break on his curveball. This was about the mental and emotional health of an athlete. Sure, often I only needed my expertise in sports psychology to aid someone struggling to compete at a high level. But sometimes my words and deeds indeed meant the difference between life and death. I could not be wrong.

I also could not be wrong as a parent. The years that launched my recovery coincided with those during which Tim and Debbie reached their late teens. They are for all that age harrowing times, a crossroad between childhood and adulthood during which decisions made affect lifetimes.

Had I been an abusive parent previous to my stay at Gateway? There is some gray area there. I never abused them physically and I do not believe I did verbally. But if it is parental abuse to drink yourself into oblivion and subject your kids to seeing you passed out in your car and not knowing if you are alive or dead, then I concede. If it is parental abuse as a narcissist to focus far more on my own desires, then I concede. If it is parental abuse to spend less time with your kids playing, conversing, and teaching, then I concede. I did not believe I was a lousy parent during my career and the four years that followed. That, however, is typical of the self-centered mindset and the fog in which I was living.

Debbie reacted as one might expect to my alcoholism. She lived with serious fear—afraid that I might get hurt or even killed. She loved me. So seeing me passed out in the car in the dead of winter was very frightening for her. So was seeing me return home covered with blood after a barroom brawl. Debbie often had no idea when I would be home and in what condition. She was forced to avoid inviting friends over in the fear that I would stumble through the door in ghastly shape. One can hardly imagine the disappointment of Debbie and Tim rarely getting a chance to accompany their father on a family outing or having one cancelled because he was out on another bender.

I had been too self-centered and out of it to realize the pain I was causing the kids. Debbie spoke about her deep concern for me every time I was late returning home, which was quite often. She became sick to her stomach with worry. She would watch for my car out the bathroom window so she could hop into bed knowing I was safe. Debbie internalized the problem, convincing herself that if she were just a good girl, I would stop drinking. That she placed one iota of blame on herself is heart wrenching. She felt as the older child that she needed to take care of the rest of the family because obviously I could not.

Yet rather than feeling a sense of anger at me for forcing that responsibility upon her, she loved me more. She protected me from myself by taking the car keys away when she knew I was drunk. When Carol Ann tried that I would fight the keys away from her. But Debbie knew I would not go after her physically because she was my princess. She has told me often how proud, happy, and relieved she felt when I began rehab. And how thankful she is today that I am still around to love.

My comeuppance had been inevitable regardless of whether I sought and received help for my addiction. My kids were destined to confront or shun me, perhaps even put me out of their minds and their lives. I am grateful they had not before my recovery. Their support helped me survive the ugliest period of my existence. They had been rightfully whisked away by Carol preceding the divorce. But they were armed and ready when the therapist at Gateway asked family members to come in to confront me. They told me how I had scared and angered them. I should have known this but my disease had disallowed it. The horrible effect I had had on my family was a revelation.

The therapy staff warned me upon my departure that the process of rekindling a loving and prosperous relationship with Debbie and Tim would not be all roses and sunshine. They explained that the family bonds that had been broken would take tremendous work on my part to repair. I had to understand that actions are far more important than words. I had made enough promises to last them a lifetime. They did not want to hear any more. I became keenly aware that I had a monumental task on my hands trying to regain their trust, love, and respect.

One way I could do that was to show interest in Tim's budding baseball career. It did not take much. The new Sam with a new perspective proved genuinely excited when his son began to display the talent that would eventually land him a professional contract. Fortunately his rise as a prospect coincided with my early recovery years. That allowed me to grow along with him.

Tim had already been exposed to both the pleasant and potentially ugly sides of the big-league lifestyle. The former was an attraction. He embraced the opportunity to soak in the clubhouse atmosphere, shake hands with the stars of the sport, watch players answer questions during post-game interviews, hear folks compare his dad to Sandy Koufax. And the dangers of celebrity life personified by me had not scared him off. If anything it buoyed his resolve during the bad old days to follow in my footsteps as an athlete but not as a man.

Early in his career at Gateway High School in Monroeville, the media placed him squarely in my shadow. Newspapers published articles referring to Tim as the son of Sam McDowell no matter how grand his own achievement on the mound. They would devote three paragraphs to me and my career then toss in a bit about Tim. But his accomplishments eventually earned Tim distinction on his own. I like to think after my recovery that I helped him become a thinking man's pitcher. The references to his dad in articles were reduced to a sentence. He would tease me about that. Five years earlier I might have felt a twinge of jealousy. Now my only emotion was pride for my son.

During my early recovery period I grew concerned that all the comparisons made by the media would hurt his confidence. Articles that featured my strikeout records and six All-Star Game appearances could have diminished his self-worth as a pitcher but he handled outside noise far better than I had at his age. He did not boast the same level of talent that I'd had. Frankly—and I can express this with complete objectivity—few have in the history of high school baseball. He was not a natural-born athlete. That is one reason that despite his accomplishments he went undrafted out of high school. But he worked his butt off to show major league potential.

Yet I refused to allow myself to fill Tim with unrealistic hope. When he pitched a strong game for Gateway, I gave him encouragement and we discussed what he did wrong. I never indicated that his mindset should be baseball-or-bust. I wanted him to aspire to reach his goals but focus on growing as a person first and understand that self-fulfillment could be achieved no matter how his professional life played out.

I reminded him that only a tiny percentage of prospects reach the majors. He played baseball and studied psychology at American University after going undrafted out of Gateway. He was setting himself up to thrive inside or outside the world of sports. I was not going to be one of those fathers who live vicariously through the achievements of their son and push mine into a baseball career. Tim appreciated me imparting a sense of realism. I remember him telling an interviewer that he had never been ashamed of me even when I was drinking. I welcomed that sentiment.

Not that I rooted against his advancement in baseball simply because I could not handle the trappings of the lifestyle as an athlete. During his time at American I spoke with him after every game. I offered my expertise on how he could maximize his talent. He had been frustrated during his first two seasons there. Tim had been an all-state pitcher at Gateway but his performance had not translated well at the college level. He had been allowing about one run per inning. He had a hard time as a freshman and sophomore pitching against seniors. So I studied his pitching motion over the summer before his junior year and advised him on taking a better mental approach to his craft. I recall working on his windup, which had become discombobulated. I visited him with a video that showed he was throwing incorrectly. I worked with him on coiling a bit more to get full extension on his windup instead of short-arming the ball to the plate.

The tutorial paid off. His velocity increased and his curveball had more snap to it. He felt smoother on the mound. And his pitching improved dramatically. His ERA fell to about one-third of what it had been his first two seasons. He required precision in his windup and delivery as well as his location because he could not fire baseballs past hitters as I had at his age or power through mistakes.

Tim was using mind over matter. He was learning to focus on every pitch, no matter the score, no matter the inning, no matter the situation. He gained an understanding of the science of pitching at around the same age as I had. Nobody had taken the reins in teaching me how to be a pitcher rather than a thrower. I was forced to learn that lesson the hard way. I refused to allow that to happen to Tim. And because I taught him that strategic approach, he began cutting down on his mistakes. During one long stretch his junior year he allowed no home runs. In one game after his adjustment he lost a 1-0 decision to George Mason, performed wonderfully in a three-hitter, yet registered no strikeouts.

Tim had forged his own identity as a pitcher, one completely different than mine. Major league scouts had begun to take notice. I had aided selflessly in his development and it made me feel great. It was all part of my transformation into a real man. And even though he never realized his dream of reaching the major leagues, he gave it his best shot, which is all any parent should ask for.

He improved to the point where he convinced the Pirates to offer him a contract in 1988. His repertoire of fastball, curve, and changeup proved effective enough to consistently retire batters in the lower minors. He moved from rookie ball to Class A in his second season and posted a fine ERA of 2.85. He was promoted to high-A for the 1990 season and performed well again but could advance no further because of the old baseball practice of giving high draft choices every chance over the lesser players irrespective of performance. His pitching under normal circumstances would have earned him another promotion. He was placed with the higher-level club in spring training but sent back to the previous level prior to breaking camp. A couple of high draft choices who had been lingering in the lower minors were moved above Tim to see if they would sink or swim. Tim asked for his release from the Pittsburgh organization but was denied. He then quit and decided to advance his second career. Three years later they still would not grant his release. That he earned a degree in psychology from Rice University and blossomed into a well-rounded person allowed Tim to avoid the struggles so many athletes face when their sports career hits a dead end.

Soon thereafter he would join me in my professional endeavor. A new and exciting venture did not await me in 1984. I had to make it happen.

15

THE TRIUMPHS
OF TRIUMPH

Anyone who pictures me skipping and smiling upon my departure from Gateway has the wrong image. A self-esteem that had reached the furthest depths one can imagine could not be raised to a healthy level in the mere twenty-eight days of an in-patient stay. The goal was to improve it through sobriety and success in the outside world.

Among my early pursuits was to launch a new career. I yearned to work in a business that motivated me. It was not selling insurance, which I had continued to do out of financial necessity. My studies in addiction and sports psychology piqued my interest. I had become an eager learner. There were no college programs teaching disease concepts at that time, nor were there any that trained students in applied sports psychology so I had to become an eager learner whenever and wherever Dr. Twerski directed me. I not only used my knowledge to help me stay sober and grow mentally and emotionally into the man I wanted to be but also to start my own company. Triumphs Unlimited was soon to become a reality.

The seeds were planted when I was a volunteer with Dr. Twerski's special groups at St. Francis. His work with addicts provided me with practical experience and a far higher level of expertise than I could have procured on my own. It was all part of my education. I liked to consider myself his protégé although it was not designed that way. I could never have approached his level of knowledge. I followed his advice and devoured books he recommended on addiction and counseling. He would then mentor me on how I could take what I read and turn it into something tangible in my life. Twerski also directed me to workshops in the field of addiction in Ohio, Pennsylvania, and West Virginia that lasted anywhere from three to ten days.

I might describe my entry into the counseling field as being lovingly coerced. Twerski was like a fisherman slowly reeling in his catch, and I was at first his very unwilling prey, fighting with every tug. I made it clear initially that I had no desire to become a counselor, in retrospect due to my belief that I was unqualified. He did not pursue the subject with me because he understood that I was resistant. But he knew quite well that I loved to learn so he continued to feed me knowledge.

Soon I began traveling with Twerski to his educational talks in different towns and suburbs around Pittsburgh. I recall one hotel at which we stayed was hosting workshops for employee assistance professionals (EAP) that also providing opportunities for certification. We arrived the day before Twerski was scheduled to speak so I decided to check out the plethora of marketing material, then walked into the ballroom to sign up for a three-hour workshop. The room was packed for the event. Upon my arrival I did not even know what an EAP was.

I learned in a hurry that it was a comparatively new science embraced by businesses to help employees whose personal problems were negatively affecting their performance and production on the job. EAPs used various methods and programs to help troubled employees. Two weeks after the workshop I received a test in the mail that I filled out and submitted. Job well done—I soon received my certification as an EAP from the State of Ohio.

I have continued to attend workshops despite my status now as formally retired. I remain so fascinated by the subject, thirsting for any new research, that I sign up from my Florida home for virtual events on new types of therapy for the addicted. I harbor no doubt that I will continue to research developments in the field until the day I die.

The eventual result of my EAP certification? Goodbye, insurance business. I had made ends meet in that field—no more, no less. It wasn't me. I felt no enthusiasm for hawking policies. My intense desire to toil in an arena of passion had been fulfilled. That achievement buoyed my self-image. I had never believed in my wildest dreams that I was smart enough or educated enough to help others. The low opinion I had held of myself for decades did not allow such a reality to come to fruition. This was a personal breakthrough.

A professor at the University of Pittsburgh suggested I incorporate Triumphs Unlimited for liability reasons and other benefits. I formed the counseling company and found a new woman—and can you believe it was another Carol? I met her through AA and eventually moved away from my parents and in with her. We lived in an extremely modest home because she was unemployed, we both had expenses, and my business had yet to take off. But soon I began making enough money to afford mortgage and utility payments. Meanwhile, a friend helped me with paperwork and advice on how to run a business. Another buddy who was an attorney aided in incorporating Triumphs Unlimited.

What helped was low rent. The town in which I decided to base my company was dying. Store fronts everywhere had signs advertising space for rent so I could practically name my price. I hired Debbie as an assistant—she had gained enough knowledge about computers and bookkeeping to be of great help. I knew nothing about computers as they started to gain importance in the workplace, and I must admit I am not much more tech savvy today.

Carol and I got married but it did not last. What did last was my new endeavor. I began promoting my counseling skills to various businesses in the Pittsburgh area. Included were hospitals, police departments, high-end stores, and unions. I was still at that time working with kids. Triumphs Unlimited did not rocket to the stratosphere. Businesspeople were skeptical. Employee assistance was still an unknown service. They had to be convinced that it would benefit their companies. I was barely scraping by. But I knew in my heart that I had something wonderful to offer. It was tough to be patient, but I stayed the course.

What was not particularly tough was staying off the booze. I found it easier than many recovering alcoholics. There were a few temptations but nothing serious. It was fortunate for me (though sad) to see others fall through the cracks and cheat on the Twelve Steps program. My three years working with Twerski and his Winners Circle group at St. Francis provided me with a wonderful perspective. I saw first hand and with a knowledge base that others dealing with addiction did not have the contrast between those who were successfully beating the habit and those who were not. I did not under any circumstances want to fall into the latter group. Watching them relapse made it easier for me to avoid temptation.

My sobriety and education in addiction and counseling could not help me in my business acumen—or lack thereof. I needed clients who believed that my expertise would prove valuable. I knew that the ideal situation for me would be work in an industry with which I was greatly familiar. The seeds for turning that dream into reality were planted one day late in 1981 when Debbie answered the phone in the little office I had set up in the back of a dress shop. On the other end was Major League Baseball Commissioner Bowie Kuhn.

Bingo!

I could hardly have been more excited about the possibility of working with ballplayers. I had not only gained vast knowledge in recent years about addiction but had been studying sports psychology since the mid-1960s. Granted, my initial foray into the subject was ignorantly motivated by a desire to reach the heart of my problems as a person when I later confronted the reality that I suffered from a disease. But delving into sports psychology did prove beneficial in gaining insight into the science of pitching and reaching levels of focus and concentration that had previously eluded me. The combination of understanding, through education and experience, addiction, sports psychology, and counseling promised great success in dealing with a wide variety of issues experienced by athletes. I also knew that baseball players would embrace me with a level of respect unearned by those who had never competed in the sport. But at the same time I knew from personal experience you cannot sell players anything—you must prove your product or idea.

Most promising was that I could impart wisdom from the school of hard knocks both as a pitcher and a person. What athletes require to thrive extends far beyond physical skills. It can be argued that the single most important ability a major leaguer needs is the ability to consistently focus. That capacity is often the difference between greatness and mediocrity among those at the same talent level. The failure of a minor leaguer to concentrate on every task at hand and successfully get the body to do what the mind tells it to do can prevent him from reaching the Show. One must boast the ability to shut out every distraction, anything unrelated to the specific pitch or at-bat or play in the field. And the mission must be attacked with confidence.

One example for a pitcher is to focus on the precise spot to throw the ball with the supreme belief that he will nail it. Attention to the process leading up to the release of the pitch is critical. Once he receives the pitch signal and location from the catcher, he must focus on how to hold the ball; placement of finger pressure; wrist and arm action; game score and situation; where runners are on base if any and their penchant for stealing; whether a ground ball, fly ball, or strike would be best; and on what side of the field the ball should ideally be hit. All of this should be second nature for major leaguers who have been hanging around mounds most of their life. The difference for the best of the best is that intense focus upon release of the ball. If that is lost, a pitcher is destined to crane his neck watching baseballs soar deep into the night.

The level of focus required by hitters is also challenging. It can be argued that the old chestnut about hitting a baseball being the toughest task in sports is true. Major league batters must understand that the weapon they wield boasts a sweet spot approximately three inches in length and two inches in width. Contact made in any other area of that bat greatly diminishes power or exit velocity. The chance for a positive result drops the further away from the sweet spot he hits the ball. So indeed sharp focus is paramount. Just as a pitcher soaks in various factors in preparation for his windup and delivery, a hitter gains awareness quickly of the set of circumstances critical to his job. How hard does the pitcher throw his fastball? How easily can I recognize his spin rate? Should I shorten my swing and focus on making hard contact with runners in scoring position? What does this pitcher like to throw with this count? And what about the contortions of my own body? Coordination, weight transfer, body turn, swing angle, where to stand in the box. Then it happens. The pitch is on its way. Focus, focus, focus. My clear understanding that the physical assistance for any player was up to the coaches allowed my mental programs to flow easier.

I recall vividly a conversation I had with Hall of Fame slugger Al Kaline, who spent his entire career with Detroit. He explained to me that he looked for nothing but the ball and how it spun. The ability to detect spin, to know in a split-second whether a fastball or slider or curve was coming his way, made Kaline a sensational hitter. He had in his lifetime swung the bat perhaps a million times. It was second nature. His success or failure on a particular pitch or at-bat was determined by his ability or inability to recognize spin and react to it. Kaline did not guess what was coming. He knew it as the ball approached the plate.

Guess hitters face greater challenges but many have thrived. Included was my former roommate, manager, and pitch-caller Joe Adcock, who often won the battle of wits against a pitcher and guessed correctly what he was about to throw. Still others can get away with virtually no thinking at the plate. They are bad-ball hitters such as Yogi Berra and Vladimir Guerrero who simply react and swing. But they too require supreme focus, perhaps more so than those who read spin or guess, because they need to concentrate on trajectory to hit the ball squarely.

The requirement of focus for fielders is more obvious and perhaps more important for one moment of distraction can mean the difference between victory and defeat. The importance of footwork and positioning cannot be overstated. But when hard grounders or line drives come whistling at an infielder or outfielder, supreme concentration is necessary. The result otherwise is runners tearing around the bases, headed for home plate.

Every player on the field must focus, and that is where I knew my background and expertise in sports psychology could help. It must be noted that all aspects of my eventual work as a counselor to athletes tied together. Performance affects everything, not just among athletes but all working people. Those who struggle on the job justifiably worry about security. Those who fret about security often allow stress to destructively affect their personal life. That can lead to the abuse of drugs and alcohol. And addiction can certainly aggravate poor performance.

I've written in earlier chapters about my living in an alcoholic fog. All people are subject to short or long periods in which they hang around in a haze.

Included are athletes. They become lazy or unconcerned with their level of concentration. Their minds become blank with no specific thought. They take their tasks for granted in their daily or professional lives. Such an approach for athletes can cost games, jobs, even careers. Mindlessness is far more common among amateurs or, specifically, among minor league baseball players. Major leaguers must be more adept at maintaining high levels of focus or they are not major leaguers for long. All athletes, however, are susceptible to lapses.

Baseball players are generally young people who often and dangerously choose to embrace a celebrity lifestyle. Meanwhile, their ability to concentrate and perform are tested several times every night. A running back in football can use poor offensive-line blocking as an excuse for failure. A basketball player can blame teammates or coaches for a lack of continuity on the court or opportunity to shine. But the spotlight on the individual in baseball provides no opportunity for blame. It has been said often that athletes must let go of what is left behind. Baseball players cannot think of the previous pitch, at-bat, or play in the field. They must concentrate only on the next one. But that is easier said than done. They can be overwhelmed by the pressure.

That is where I would enter the picture. All I needed was a chance. The phone call from Kuhn at least appeared to have opened that door for me.

16

RESISTANCE AND ACCEPTANCE

The Kuhn call came out of left field. Little did I know he had grown concerned about addiction in major league baseball and was contemplating the idea of launching a program to combat the problem. But combating the problem was not the only problem.

What became clear to me was that neither Kuhn nor anyone else running the league felt any motivation to include alcohol in the equation. Addiction to them meant drugs and only drugs. The fact that players might be alcoholics—given a lifestyle that encourages drinking—either escaped their attention or was purposely ignored. I tend to believe the latter. Major league baseball had for generations promoted a relationship with alcohol manufacturers through advertising. Baseball, hot dogs, and apple pie? It was more like baseball, hot dogs, and beer. This was the early 1980s. And Harry Caray was not hawking lemonade during broadcasts. He was peddling Budweiser. Beer commercials have remained tied to baseball for nearly a century.

My rekindled relationship with the game started a bit more than a decade after I retired as a pitcher. Kuhn, who would be replaced as commissioner in 1984 by Peter Ueberroth, called me to discuss a counseling program for addicted players. Based on the absence of any such treatment during my career and what I had gathered since, I knew one was needed. I also understood that despite my absence from the game, my legend as a boozer lived on within the sport. So Kuhn, who had served as commissioner for the last six years of my playing career, was certainly familiar with my reputation on both ends of the spectrum. Not only did he recall that I was the most violent drunk in baseball, he knew that I had turned my life around and begun to counsel others on addiction. He had become aware after reading an article in the *Pittsburgh Press* that spotlighted my recovery and education in the field.

I relished the opportunity to help. I told Kuhn that I would design a program that could stem the tide but warned him that it would take time. My obligations to attend AA meetings and to my continued education through Dr. Twerski remained priorities. In addition I was still in the waning years of my career selling insurance. But I did put my best effort into a written proposal that I sent to the commissioner three weeks later. His reply: Thanks, but no thanks. My program included counseling for players with alcohol problems, and he wanted nothing to do with it.

I was not surprised. I suspected as I started the project that major league baseball would avoid tackling that issue like Superman avoided Kryptonite. I understood that advertising revenue from the alcohol industry would prove more important than ridding alcoholic players of their disease. Today beer and liquor advertisers warn folks to drink responsibly. But this was still a play-hard, drink-hard period in baseball. Drunkenness was snickered at rather than taken with the gravity it deserves. It was considered to some a sign of manliness. Kuhn, in fact, released a statement claiming that baseball did not have an alcohol problem. So the response was just as I expected.

What I did not expect arrived a year later via another phone call, this one from Texas Rangers president Mike Stone and new general manager Joe Klein. What I had created for Kuhn circulated around the baseball grapevine and eventually motivated their inquiry. I remained skeptical of intent regarding their desire to target alcoholism as well as drug addiction but I was certainly pleased when they invited me to spring training. They wanted to witness my interaction with their players and discuss the possibility of implementing a program for the Rangers.

My first task when speaking with Stone and Klein, as well as minor league director Tom Grieve, was to make certain they understood that my work was educational and not punitive. Our conversation certainly piqued the interest of Stone, an attorney whose wife had toiled for two decades as a psychologist in the addiction field. Then our meeting came to a crossroads, one that I knew had to be reached. I informed them in no uncertain terms that I planned to address alcohol as well as other drugs. I feared that the Rangers had adopted the same policy as major league baseball and would shun the idea.

That suspicion remained when they allowed me to talk with the players. I revealed to the players immediately that management was watching so if they preferred to speak with me in private I would be glad to meet them in my motel. I told them not to take my word for anything but allow me to prove my sincerity and ability to help. I designed my talk to deal primarily with the feelings, physical cost, emotions, and changes associated with drug and alcohol abuse. I yearned to prove my expertise on the subject and make clear its impact on their on-field performance. I realized that the players were skeptical despite their knowledge of my personal experiences in the game. They knew I had been a drunk during my playing days but that alone meant nothing because young people, including ballplayers, are always being told something and often they perceive it as bullshit. So I had to convince them that what I offered had value and could help them perform. They were not going to stop drinking or using drugs simply because I talked with them.

Mission accomplished. It mattered not that the brass openly observed which players offered to converse individually. Eleven players indeed came down to the field from the stands to speak with me. Some had questions about the facts I had imparted. Others simply wanted to confirm that my understanding about alcohol and drug abuse within the sport had great merit. Many admitted to dealing with such issues but never fully understanding the direct or indirect connection to physical performance regarding stamina, breathing, speed, bat speed, mound control, or balance as a hitter or pitcher as well as the mental effects such as fear, defensiveness, and self-doubt. The players told me that they knew immediately what I was talking about.

Two days later I spoke to them as a group about sports psychology and the effects they would experience at various points throughout the season. This time most of the players came down to discuss that subject further. I emphasized strongly that all individual conversations had to be made private and that they could contact me at the motel. During the ten days that followed I had appointments nearly every hour after workouts until 9 p.m. I found it interesting that the management team, which was staying in the same motel, could see their players coming to me. Some in management asked me to dinner but my full schedule disallowed it.

I left after those ten days had passed. I thanked the Rangers for the opportunity. Stone was impressed enough with my work to call me two weeks later. Rangers management embraced a progressive approach to a problem that was as old as baseball itself. Historians of the sport have researched ballplayers from before the turn of the twentieth century who struggled with alcohol addiction. Yet drunkenness had been either swept under the rug or accepted as part of the old "Boys will be boys" syndrome.

Grieve had come to grips with the dangers and decided to do something about it. He detected something different about my approach and gave me encouragement. He scheduled me for a talk with his minor leaguers three days later that went well. Klein eventually called me and asked me to formulate a counseling plan and contract for his organization. I designed the latter so the club could cancel me at their discretion. I understood that if management and players did not believe I was making a positive difference I could not ethically continue to work with them. But I was confident I would.

My proposal was to visit the major league club and each of the farm teams once a year then offer more of my time if they so desired as they shared results of the first talk with me. I would implement a two-fold plan of sports psychology and employee assistance that included both drug and alcohol prevention. One stipulation insisted upon was suspension without pay of players unwilling to help themselves through my proposed resolutions or referrals. The level of abuse would dictate the solution. I did not foresee any problems in this area. Players and management understood the importance of staying on the field and producing. This was especially true among minor leaguers and unproven Rangers. Their future was at stake. They had yet to cash in on the multimillion-dollar contracts being offered by that time. Time was of the essence, however. Circumstances dictated that I could not wait until the offseason to start therapy.

So successful were my efforts that the Rangers asked me to increase my workload the following year. From that season forward they wanted me to visit with all their teams for one-week periods every month, including spring training and instructional league periods in the winter. Their players were impressed enough that they began to spread the word about my work to peers in other organizations. They especially embraced my sports-psychology program because they connected it to improved performance on the field. Not only were current Texas players benefiting from my program, the organization began acquiring personnel that other clubs could no longer control and turning them over to me to send their careers and lives in a positive direction.

The players who chose to benefit from my counsel were assured of privacy in our discussions. Usually one or two would seek me out after I spoke to a group. I would never meet with them in the clubhouse but rather arranged to advise them in one of our hotel rooms after the game. I would estimate that 40 percent of the issues revolved around drugs, alcohol, or different emotional problems. The rest wanted my assistance on performance enhancement. That did not mean I was giving them pointers on how to grip a slider or close what had been an open stance in the batter's box. My advice revolved around improving focus and concentration.

Among my points was that drinking affected those necessary elements of performance success. I never told a player to completely abstain from alcohol unless it had been determined he was an alcoholic. Drinking is a socially accepted practice. And occasionally a player will consume a bit too much. He may not necessarily get drunk, but perhaps catch a little buzz. In such cases I asked them to be sensitive to how they felt and thought the next day, especially during a game. Were they tired? Were they weak? Did they experience a change in their breathing? Most important was their mental state. Self-doubt might have snuck in, maybe a little fear.

Those negative emotions affect focus and concentration and I believe cut ability in half. That can seriously threaten a career. The mind can only handle one thought at a time, especially when a keen level of concentration is necessary during competition. One should replace the fear of what might happen with the confidence of what can be achieved. The game otherwise becomes more challenging. A hitter in that state of mind might be unduly intimidated by the pitcher's abilities. Those thoughts intensify and become a greater obstacle the more a person drinks or uses what they consider performance-enhancing drugs.

Counseling in the sports psychology realm requires far more immediacy than working with addiction problems. Some situations reached a level of complexity that forced me to turn an athlete over to a specialist but there was little time for long, drawn-out therapy because that athlete could in the meantime lose his spot on the team or even his career. Even in cases of abuse or addiction, reality therapy was the quickest method of luring a player into recognizing his behavior as destructive. Once that negative influence was proven to the athlete, he could turn it around.

One example spotlighted a player who exhibited immature behavior and tended to over-celebrate. I sat down with him and we reflected on what was happening to his body and mind: his mental condition, his joint tiredness, his negative thoughts regarding performance. I challenged him to test my expertise after the next game. It became obvious immediately that he understood where I was coming from. Two weeks later he sidled up and thanked me. He had proven me right to himself. He vowed never to party again. The player stopped drinking throughout that season and I noticed the same abstinence the following spring.

These were the issues players wanted to discuss with me more than any other during my decades as a counselor. I would also explain the effect of alcohol from a more technical standpoint, such as what happens chemically from the time it hits the throat and stomach and is absorbed into the intestines and blood system as well as its effect the brain. It is quite a disruptive process. The warning to players was clear. They could imagine a negative impact that was perhaps fifty times stronger or more with an alcoholic or drug addict trying to compete at a high level.

I worked with the Rangers from 1983 to 1998. But free rein to impart my wisdom and experience varied. The club changed managers often and a couple of them worried that I was infringing on their territory. They wanted to be the sole motivators and sports psychologists for their players despite my training and experience in those areas. One told me he simply did not have time for me to speak with his group. He asked me to write down a transcript of my talk. And in the same amount of time it would have taken me to give the speech, he gave it himself. His ego had gotten in the way.

Dealing with resistance became a constant battle. But it was worthwhile knowing that it was a winning one. Those who either did not understand the value of my work or jealously took steps to hinder my relationships with teams and players were fighting a losing game. They were like a snowstorm and I was like the postman. Nothing was going to stop me from making my appointed rounds as the first counselor in professional sports history.

17

EXPANDING MY
HORIZONS

The reach of Sam McDowell the counselor had grown by 1986. That was the year I took a call from the Toronto organization, whose players had received positive feedback from their peers with Texas, which gave the Blue Jays permission to speak with me. I met with the entire management team during spring training, including the president and CEO, general manager, doctor, minor league director, and two scouts. I detailed what I offered as a counselor as well as contract provisions and informed them that I was quite willing to speak with the Rangers about splitting time between the two teams.

I was taken aback when their minor league director and major league pitching coach asked me if I could help their pitchers with their physical approach and performance on the mound. It amounted to a coaching task that I rejected because I required in my work as a counselor a boundary between me and the players. Mixing in advice about emotional or substance problems with how to snap off a 12-to-6 curveball would not only blur my relationship with pitchers but usurp the authority of the coaches within the organization. It would also have watered down the serious nature of my program.

Soon I was working for both Texas and Toronto. My philosophy and approach had been well established by then. I understood that every player I counseled had problems that were unique to his life and career. But I also knew that in the realm of sports psychology I could not allow athletes to dwell on the past. I directed their focus to the next pitch or play.

Sometimes I used humor to lighten the mood. At one point I had spoken with the Triple-A Syracuse Chiefs about how to erase negative images. A pitcher named Alex Sanchez, who eventually earned a cup of coffee with the

Blue Jays, certainly needed my advice after allowing eight runs, including three home runs, before a fourth-inning knockout in a lopsided defeat. "Did you hear about the commotion over at the bus station last night during the game?" I asked him in reference to a terminal located about 250 feet beyond the center-field fence. "They heard all those home-run balls hitting the roof and thought it was sniper fire."

Some who did not understand my objective might have perceived my words as mocking but the intent was to add levity to the situation and prevent the loss from getting Sanchez down. It reinforced a lecture I'd given the previous day.

My approach worked and brought me tremendous pride. All but 4 of the 175 ballplayers I counseled during the late 1980s and early 1998s actively worked to recover from their addiction and two that relapsed returned to me for further treatment. One of my successes was Pirates minor league pitcher Mike York, whose story was told in a 1990 issue of *Sports Illustrated* feature that spotlighted my recovery and work with ballplayers. We met when he was just twenty-two years old in 1986. Despite his youth he feared that he had drunk himself out of baseball after he had been released by the Yankees, White Sox, and Tigers due to his alcoholism.

I had been dispatched to Pirate City for the start of instructional league and had begun presenting educational seminars on addiction, prevention, and sports psychology. The instructional league season was about to begin. One evening Syd Thrift told me about his conversation with scouts who were impressed by York's talent and knew he was available after alcoholism had cost him jobs with three teams. Thrift asked me to meet with York and determine whether I could help him. He did not want to waste a contract on a lost cause.

My initial meeting with York proved promising enough that I endorsed him. But that recommendation came with a caveat. I told Thrift that York needed recovery time before being placed on the field. No dice. Thrift stuck a Pirates uniform on him and sent him out to pitch. His first two outings were disastrous. He became so angry after one performance that he flew into a rage and fired the ball into the outfield when the coach arrived to remove him from the game. Thrift arrived the next day and threatened to send York home. I offered instead to talk to the kid for a couple more days and reminded Thrift that I urged the Pirates not to sign him yet.

Soon I was confronting York. I called him a drunk and described all his excuses as bullshit. I was seeking to draw out his anger and succeeded. He rose from his chair ready to fight. I told him to sit the Hell down and I pointed to his chair. And as I headed out the door I expressed my satisfaction that he had gotten mad, informing him that I was on my way to recommend that the Pirates sign him to a contract for the following year but only if he met my requirements. If he did not attend an in-patient rehab clinic for twenty-eight days, call me every other night at a specific time while there, attend counseling sessions near his home upon his release and AA meetings every night until spring training the following March, and stay in contact with me, he would be waived by the Pirates. He had no choice. Had he not accepted his career would've been over. I placed all the stipulations in a contract.

York embraced my challenge. He spent a month at a rehab center in Florida, calling me every night for advice and moral support. I did not always tell him what he wanted to hear. I believed if I made it too easy on him he would revert to his old habits. And he did not as we continued to work nightly all winter.

During that winter I also updated Thrift on York's progress. I predicted that York would thrive that spring but warned Thrift about possible mishaps. I strongly urged Thrift to keep York at the same minor league level at which he had started because relocation during his initial recovery period could prove to be a damaging jolt to his recovery. A sober York soared to the heights in 1987 in Class-A ball. He compiled a 17-6 record and struck out more than a batter per inning. Thrift twice asked me if he could promote York but I requested he refrain, and Thrift complied until he moved York up to pitch in the playoffs.

York appeared destined for greatness. He performed well consistently and continued to rise in the Pittsburgh organization. He boasted a curveball that dropped off the table. But an ignorant pitching coach ruined his career. He changed York's delivery to make his Uncle Charlie start at the hitter and break over the plate rather than drop straight down. When a pitcher has for his entire life thrown a 12-to-6 curve and the delivery is altered, he begins to use entirely different muscle groups. The change can be made eventually but not instantly, and certainly not in intense game situations.

The result was an arm injury that forced York's career to stagnate once he reached the majors. York pitched well for Pittsburgh during a brief stint in 1990 then got traded to Cleveland, where he struggled the following year. After that, he would never play in another big-league game. Even so, like many of the athletes I have counseled, York became a lifelong friend.

My goal as a counselor to athletes was to achieve fast and long-lasting results. My therapy required speedy and permanent solutions as athletes have no time to waste. They must produce *now* because careers are short and sometimes there are no tomorrows. So whether their issue is addiction, confidence, or struggling to focus, I had to be Mr. Fix-It Fast. I devised a method of counseling that I called "keying in, locking, loading, and firing." It was intended to combat negative thinking. I would tell a player whose failures had brought up pessimism to focus on pleasant imagery, such as his wife or girlfriend in a bikini on a warm, wind-swept beach, then maintain that positivity in concentrating on the task at hand on the field.

I did not respond to pessimism with sugary optimism. I provided a permanent method for players to help themselves. The solution worked faster in the cases of athletic performance than addiction. I waved no magic wand that could bring sobriety. I knew from painful experience that it takes time, grit, determination, and intense desire to rid oneself of that insidious disease.

That is why, for instance, AA promotes its Twelve Steps program. If it is followed faithfully, it works. During my forty years working in the field of addiction I've seen miracles as well as tragedies, preventable sadness, depression, and divorce. I have witnessed inexplicable phenomena. I saw them with professional athletes early in my career and everyday people later. But what was confirmed to me was that the most effective and lasting method of beating this disease is the Twelve Steps program but only for those who buy in. Its value is negated by those who cheat, partially accept, refuse, or pretend to work and live it.

I know athletes who embraced the program. Their careers took off like rockets. The positive changes in their outlook and performance were obvious. One did not need to be a psychologist or therapist to see the difference. Many scouts would tell me that they were watching a new and improved player. But faking the program is known in the field of addiction as "white knuckling." Those who merely feign adherence live in a malaise. They just exist, constantly seeking attention with superficial rather than real changes such as in hair color, tattoos, body piercing, or shifts in attitude, such as acting like a know-it-all.

The good news is that many who tire of living a fake life finally take the program seriously. The changes within them occur so subtly and slowly that they often do not recognize them, but their friends and family members do. Eventually they feel happier and have a sense of inner peace. They seek respect by accomplishing things, excelling at their job, even attacking personal or professional goals they had at one time considered unattainable. I once followed the travails of a waiter who gained so much success through the Twelve Steps program that he transformed himself into a highly successful businessman.

Most important in my personal life was that I had moved from the fast lane into a more peaceful ride. I was once driven to impress others. Now I was toiling quietly to impress myself. I worked out of a modest office in Swissvale, a hilly suburb of Pittsburgh overlooking the Monongahela River and Interstate 376. Small gold letters on the front window of my Triumphs Unlimited office read, Sudden Sam McDowell & Associates, Counselors for Professional Athletes and Athletic Teams. There was nothing flashy about me or my business. I had gained emotional security. Throughout my entire second career I refused any and all notoriety. I refused hundreds of radio or TV interviews. (There were rare exceptions when the writer went ahead and did his story anyway despite my wishes.) My program was confidential and I greatly preferred that players not think otherwise because of negative or even positive publicity regarding their issues. That I eschewed publicity was quite a departure from the old Sudden Sam.

Not that I had time to sit around and twiddle my thumbs. Inquiries about my services from major league organizations eventually totaled seven. Two National Hockey League franchises and one National Football League club also expressed an interest. I worked one year with the Chicago Cubs and Cincinnati Reds, the latter team after a request from a friend. One convenient option I chose to pursue was the Pirates. But I was forced to turn most teams down. I simply did not want to spread myself too thin because I believed it would weaken my effectiveness in helping individual athletes. I was already on the road forty weeks out of the year. At any time I might be working with several sports figures on a case-by-case basis. And I spent hours upon hours planning my visits. I kept a map of North America in my office with destinations marked in bright colors. The schedule left me little time for me and my family.

Meanwhile I had to battle the perception that persists even today that I only worked with alcoholics. My counseling had branched out to a wide range of emotional, psychological, and family problems. It required levels of experimentation on my part while trying to avoid trial and error because mistakes can be costly when dealing with human lives. Moreover one must realize that a certain type of depression is the natural byproduct of alcoholism and drug addiction. I learned during my years as a counselor that major league players can often hide or at least deal with their depression partly because they have already reached the primary goal of their life and some of the career pressure has been lifted. Such is not the case with minor leaguers, who can be overwhelmed by depression, even though they might not be aware of it, leading to the end of their career.

Sometimes I felt consumed by my counseling. My obsessive-compulsive nature did not disappear along with my addiction. I acquired more counseling credits than necessary to maintain my certification. Rather than read books featuring subject matter outside the realm of my business, I pored over medical thrillers and self-help manuals. I read *Think & Grow Rich* by Napoleon Hill so many times that I could recite passages from it. The good news was that by the early 1990s I had cut my cigarette habit in half to one and one-half packs a day. Soon thereafter I was smoke-free—no butts.

My limited free time beyond working and reading was spent either at the golf course with friends or dabbling in art, which had become a passion. I enjoyed painting and still do, mostly forest scenes, landscapes, and seascapes. I was constantly moving forward in my professional and personal life after walking around in a fog nearly forty years. And I welcomed the new challenges ahead.

18

GOING TO BAT

It was 1993. I was in a hotel room when the phone rang. On the other end was Joe Garagiola, former big-league catcher who gained greater fame as an analyst on nationally televised baseball broadcasts. He sounded distressed.

Garagiola had received a call from Hall of Fame pitcher Ferguson Jenkins, who had spoken with former Red Sox left-hander Bill Lee. Garagiola initially contacted former Dodgers great Don Newcombe, who declined to intervene because he lacked training. Garagiola informed me that a one-time teammate of Lee was trying to commit suicide and asked me if I could help. I offered my willingness to try. He then revealed who was attempting to end his life. It was Bernie Carbo, who was known publicly as a free spirit during his twelve years in the league—mostly as a platoon hitter with power but he was also a drug addict. There is no free spirit among those in the clutches of addiction.

In 1975, Carbo had made history with a three-run homer for Boston in Game 6 of perhaps the greatest World Series battle ever. He later admitted to having been high when he took that fateful swing of the bat. Now he was on the verge of ending it all by locking himself in his garage and suffocating on car exhaust fumes.

There was no time to waste. I had to talk Carbo off the proverbial ledge. I stressed that there was a future for him with a window of light. I was able to stabilize him, calm him down, and eventually convince him to get professional help. I called Carbo the next day with details, he checked into a rehab facility I set up, and he eventually recovered. An anxiety attack at one point forced a transfer from the rehab center to a hospital, but I met with Carbo a short time following his release. During his stay he had met a pastor who gave him a spiritual perspective that helped him fully recover. Carbo went on to become a minister, and he now works with at-risk children.

I had learned long before that though millions of people suffer from the same addictions—alcohol or drugs—each of their stories is unique and must be addressed individually. The seeds of Carbo's addiction had been planted well before he played major league baseball. One might have assumed that smashing a home run in a World Series that has forever held a special place in the hearts and minds of Red Sox fans would have brought Carbo joy, at least at that moment. But he was miserable. He struggled with deep insecurities as I did during my career. He believed his father did not like him yet he could not stop seeking his father's approval. His marriage was falling apart. He argued incessantly with his managers and coaches.

Carbo continued to abuse drugs while running a hair salon in Michigan after retiring. He began using cocaine when that became popular. His mother, who was devastated by her son's addiction, committed suicide in 1989. He blamed his father but in his heart took personal responsibility for her death. His dad died three months later. Carbo then moved to Florida to play in a senior league.

He hoped a new lifestyle would result in positive changes but both he and his wife remained in the vice of drug abuse. One day he came to the realization that he was a dead man if he did not kick the habit. And since his wife refused to change, he kicked his marriage and filed for divorce. But even that did not produce the desired results. Carbo moved on to even harder drugs and drank heavily as well. A second marriage proved tumultuous and disastrous. That led to the suicide attempt.

It would not be the last life-taking threat in which I intervened. It was, however, the one that received the most publicity during my time with the Baseball Assistance Team, from which I have officially retired. The organization, known appropriately as BAT, was launched by Major League Baseball Commissioner Peter Ueberroth in 1987. By that time a group of former players who had become increasingly concerned by poverty among their peers asked Ueberroth to begin a help program. He agreed and set up funding through donations from insurance companies, one of which funded an old-timers' game that raised about $10 million over three years.

My work with BAT began six months after its introduction. My most harrowing cases involved suicide because they had to be handled immediately and delicately, yet firmly. I was responsible for talking players through nineteen live suicide threats and others in which the athletes were considered suicidal. I initially provided a list of counselors I believed could help the newly formed organization without the intent of being among them. Garagiola, who was among the founders of BAT, ripped the list up and insisted that I join the group. I agreed to serve as a volunteer for one year. Three decades later I was still swinging for the fences for BAT.

I am proud to have been the first EAP counselor in the history of professional sports. And BAT is easily the most comprehensive EAP in American society. It has expanded greatly over the years to help any former player, family member, umpire, minor leaguer, or front-office worker experiencing problems whether financial, emotional, psychological, or even educational. Among the personal issues tackled by BAT counselors are addiction and severe family conflicts. My son Tim later took over my duties and, as a trained psychologist, was able to expand its services exponentially.

The program has been an unqualified success. BAT boasts an 85 percent success rate of recovery regarding drug or alcohol abuse as well as psychological or emotional problems. The organization gained such a fine reputation that former NFL, NBA, and NHL players asked us to help their colleagues because those leagues had fallen woefully short in what they considered their obligations to their alumni.

I found it interesting and rewarding working strictly with retired athletes and baseball personnel for BAT. The contrast was striking as I continued to counsel active players for individual major league organizations. Among my challenges with BAT was working with the children of coaches or managers. The parents reported that their kids were suffering from depression and requested intervention. They informed me of red flags that had convinced them that their offspring were in trouble. Some had threatened to take their lives—the rate of suicide among youth had skyrocketed in recent years. Warnings from parents proved critical because they allowed me to intervene in time. My job was to calm and stabilize the child and provide the most appropriate referral in that city to take over the case immediately.

The process in cases of threatened suicide must be adhered to strictly. Upon learning of a suicide attempt, I would notify the local emergency medical services as soon as I knew the address of the distressed individual. I gained as much knowledge as quickly as possible over the phone to assess the level of despair, depression, and hopelessness the individual was experiencing. I listened intently for all the warning signs. It was important that I maintain a soft, melodic tone in my voice during our discussion—any expression of shock or excitement could have proven dangerous.

I understood entering a conversation that the distressed might not want to talk. I was also aware up front that a suicidal person has lost all hope of overcoming his or her roadblocks and is convinced there is no way out, no solution, no door through which to escape. So I had to keep the dialogue flowing and utilize the entire spectrum of fact-finding questions. I could not be fearful of using the word "suicide" often because the severity and finality of what was being threatened could not be overstated. It was my job to convince those in such a frantic state to calm down and embrace the feeling that their lives remained valuable—they had to see a light at the end of a dark tunnel, to know that there was a tomorrow. The suicidal needed to recognize that even if there seemed to be no immediate solution to the problem that was causing them such distress, there is always a solution and a purpose in life.

What I wish everyone would understand is that we are all unique and we are all special. And when I dealt with suicide attempts or ideation, I was confronted with very individual and often complex personal dramas in which people found themselves in positions from which escape seemed impossible. So I went with the flow. I allowed the person to dictate my final approach. I was keen on the complete spectrum of suicide. I began seeking to lure suffering individuals into conversations to talk about their feelings of misery or at least their situation and thinking. It should be noted, though, that I never worked with female athletes in depression and addiction. I considered myself unqualified for a myriad of reasons.

The referral system through the United States, Puerto Rico, and the Dominican Republic that I created for my work as a counselor was critical to ensuring the best possible outcome. I could not be at more than one place at a time, and issues with players elsewhere sometimes necessitated intervention. I sought confidentiality for players and coaches with problems then offered solutions that involved referrals to skilled professionals. But those who required help in the sports-psychology realm needed me on site so I could personally work with them.

Sometimes during my years toiling with major league baseball organizations I was forced to fight through barriers to simply receive access to a player. In those cases, the benefits of my expertise were not fully recognized or appreciated. Such was a greater problem early in my career before what was considered a new direction in player interaction and intervention had been established.

One case involved a player for Triple-A Oklahoma City with a serious drug problem. The Rangers had acquired him from another club that did not want to deal with his worsening addiction. I insisted that he needed to be placed in a rehabilitation center immediately and the player agreed. Of course I had to mention this to team management because it was rare that I would ask to send a player away during the season as it placed a media and public spotlight on the individual and threatened to hurt his standing with the organization. So to avoid widespread knowledge of my desire, I requested an audience only with Texas minor league director Marty Scott. I knew he had complete faith in me and had mentioned that he would go along with whatever I thought was necessary to protect a player.

Then came a roadblock. Somehow a physician learned of my intention and met with the player himself in private. He decided to take charge of the situation and send the player to a friend who was a psychologist, many of whom do not treat addiction for what it is—a disease. I was upset upon learning of what I deemed a dangerous rejection or circumvention of my assessment and recommendation. But the Rangers decided otherwise. The player visited the psychologist weekly during homestands and every two weeks that winter.

The plan backfired. He soon called me in a desperate state of depression. He begged for help, and I provided it without informing the Rangers. I had him placed in a rehab center for a month, set up weekly counseling upon his graduation, and sought to ensure that he would follow the Twelve Steps program religiously. The happy ending to this story features sobriety, a stint in the major leagues, and a peaceful and productive retirement.

I was often encouraged or forced over the years to step aside and allow team physicians, medical directors, or orthopedic surgeons take the lead in a treatment with which I disagreed. I did so with little argument. But I cannot recall one case in which a player received significant help from a psychiatrist, psychologist, or medical doctor. There was little I could do. I had to back off without a challenge.

And sometimes I fight myself over it. I periodically allowed interventions to happen throughout my career as an EAP and counselor knowing that the best interest for the athlete would not be served. I estimate ten situations in which I retreated from carrying out what I knew to be the most effective approach by accepting the demands of a doctor, psychologist, or team official. These situations all occurred during my first five years as an EAP and counselor as I was intimidated by these medical professionals.

It still hurts. A clean, sober life remained elusive for every ballplayer forced into that path. I recall one doctor sending a player to a psych rehab center three times despite my insisting that those in the facility were not trained to help with addiction and that the player would fail to receive the necessary help. And now that player bounces back and forth from sobriety to drunkenness. Folks can still read in the newspaper about his DUI, cocaine possession charge, or other trouble with the law.

One should not assume from these experiences that I feel a lack of reverence for psychologists, psychiatrists, and physicians in general. Quite the opposite. Throughout my years as a ballplayer and counselor I had a difficult time with some in those fields because I respected them so much that it interfered with my own knowledge, research, and understanding. I bowed to their judgment. I allowed myself to get so close to particular doctors that they asked me to call them by their given name rather than their professional name but I could not even bring myself to do that because I was so impressed by the sacrifices they made personally and educationally. Out of respect I simply call them "Doc." Their work still reminds me of my desire in high school to pursue a medical career before the lucrative baseball offers arrived that made it virtually impossible to take that long and arduous path.

But the medical world is not without its con artists or at least those who are ineffective in treatment. What many people do not know is that some publicly advertised rehab centers and recovery programs have been designed by alcoholics or drug addicts who did not like certain aspects of the Twelve Steps program, particularly those requiring self-honesty. Those who research these programs will learn that they fail to secure long-term sobriety. They work well for about six months but they do not help addicts stay clean.

Statistics have proven that AA and its affiliates such as Narcotics Anonymous and Gamblers Anonymous boast the highest percentage of recovery for short-term and long-term addicts. All three embrace a program that has proven for decades to provide the strongest possibility for recovery. AA's medical model includes 30-day, 60-day, and 90-day stays in rehab centers or a three-year program. I defy anyone to find bona fide, objective research refuting my contention that no other medical model compares to that of AA for sustained success even though a new twist in recovery programs seems to rear its ugly head just about every year. Almost all of them come from California and most of them patronize the alcoholic or the drug addict to secure big money for their rehabilitation process.

I recognized then and do today that bucking the system would have been difficult and would have threatened my relationship with the organizations I served, thereby preventing me from helping other ballplayers. But it still amazes me the number of medical professionals who do not understand alcoholism and drug addiction.

I vowed when I began working with BAT to help athletes with all my heart and soul. I had experienced the pain of losing a great career, and I would be damned if I would allow another player to throw away his if I could do anything about it. During my first twenty-eight years counseling athletes with addiction problems for BAT, I can proudly report only six permanent relapses. That level of success is unmatched but does not indicate smooth sailing from the start. About 40 percent of those who went through our program relapsed, usually once, but returned to BAT for help and were given the opportunity to follow our recovery program again and to the letter. One important reason for this level of success was our constant monitoring system. We remain to this day in touch with hundreds of recovering players and their family members, with whom we have worked for twenty-six years. I am personally still in touch with many former players from the various teams I spent time with.

The BAT program is simple. Like the sport itself, we feature two different leagues of play. One begins when a player comes to us for help that is strictly financial. Our executive director will then meet with the grant committee to study the situation and determine whether a donation is warranted. The other scenario is an alcohol, drug, emotional, psychological, or family problem—sometimes a combination of more than one. Those cases, which often also require financial assistance, were turned over to me before my retirement. It was my job to find a solution.

Several considerations arose. One was the level of seriousness of the situation. Did it require immediate attention? And what would that entail? My next task was to evaluate the individual and determine his specific problem, addiction or otherwise, so he could be either properly placed at a rehab center in the city in which he lived or in the cases of emotional or psychological issues that did not warrant changes in living environment, scheduled for weekly appointments with professionals I knew and trusted. Because of changes in the rehabilitation field, we now send those who require treatment to rehabs we know are successful and maintain certain specific modalities. We are not interested in fancy, patronizing programs designed to grab the suffering only to make money and the Hell with their actual recovery.

My relationship with the ballplayer did not end there. Follow-up was critical. I continued to monitor progress through reports from the rehab facility to ensure that he was taking the process seriously. I demanded after graduation that he attend nightly self-help meetings and adhere to the program. He also had to keep appointments with any psychiatrist, psychologist, marriage counselor, or other professional I deemed most appropriate based on the diagnosed problem. But what was most important for these recovering alcoholics and drug addicts to realize was that skimping on the program ensured failure while doing the opposite guaranteed success. It was that simple.

Though I have retired, I remain a BAT board member. I have said often that my work for BAT was the most rewarding of my life. I remain friends with many of those I helped recover. And I still follow the action on the field. I want the sport to be as healthy and vibrant as those individuals who are now living fruitful and happy lives. But I do not like what I have been seeing in recent years.

19

A WHOLE NEW
BALLGAME

The year escapes me but it was the late 1980s or early 1990s. I had begun working with the Texas Rangers. Manager Bobby Valentine had invited to spring training arguably the greatest pitcher in history, Sandy Koufax.

One day I was standing in the hallway drinking my morning coffee and talking with Valentine. Soon one of the team's top pitchers walked in and noticed Koufax sitting in the coach's office reading a newspaper.

"Who is that?" he asked.

Valentine rolled his eyes.

"That's Sandy Koufax," I replied incredulously.

"Who is that?" repeated the pitcher.

Koufax was like Dick Clark—he never seemed to age. His playing career had ended a quarter-century earlier but he looked like he could still be firing peas from the mound. I wondered at first how he was not recognized. Then I was shocked that any major league pitcher would not know his name. Ultimately I was saddened by what I saw as an indictment of the modern-day player.

Times had changed. It was not just baseball. The lack of appreciation among athletes for the history of their sport had become apparent. It grew at the same rate salaries grew. Most players in my era did not bother asking, "What's in it for me?" because before the advent of free agency they knew the answer. They received a contract from the club in the mail and signed it or, on rare occasions, held out for a bit more. Thanks to Marvin Miller—today's players should be whispering thanks to him daily but many probably don't recognize his name either—salary figures soon began exploding to the point that now some guys earning $15-$25 million a year are considered underpaid. I would never blame any player for maximizing his earning potential. But the negative effect on the game itself makes me a bit sad.

What negative effect? The drive for the almighty buck has greatly impacted how a hitter approaches his at-bats and, in turn, the mindset of the pitcher. The change has proven monumental. Player agents, who have tremendous influence, stress that only the big boppers make big money. They strongly encourage their clients to swing for the fences. I have witnessed, first hand, players ignoring calls for sacrifices from their manager and swinging away. The pecking order in major league baseball has changed along with the salary structure. Established players not only try to hit for power, they have more power than their managers. And pitchers, all of whom realize that hitters practice far less plate discipline, use their split-finger fastballs and downward breaks on sliders to induce swings and misses on balls that do not even reach the catcher.

Major league baseball was forced to look itself in the mirror after the labor dispute and work stoppage of 1994 that wiped out the World Series and turned off the nation. Resentful fans were staying home in droves. Then, with steroids legal and even after they became illegal, behemoths on the field began luring folks back to the ballpark and creating interest in the game again by slugging pitches deep into the night at a prodigious rate, shattering single-season and career home-run records set by players who had achieved them without performance-enhancing drugs.

The league has been accused of urging Rawlings in recent years to manufacture baseballs that will travel farther in the belief that fans love the long ball, which seemed true in the steroid era but not necessarily anymore. What fans want is action, and the home run concludes with hitters simply jogging around the bases. When teams hit three hundred home runs in a season, as did the Twins in 2019, it becomes monotonous.

And pitchers know when and why the ball has been altered. When one handles a baseball thousands of times every season, he gains a sensitivity to the touch in his fingers and fingertips. One must understand that every ball is hand-stitched, and they are going to be different. Pitchers can feel it. I recall that raised stitches were ideal for throwing a sharper curve because they offered more friction. Smoother balls with inverted stitching were better for fastballs. Some balls had bumps in the cover or stitching. During my active career I knew of two pitchers who had balls examined and both times the balls were found to be altered. Baseballs can be harder or softer or lighter. But what has become obvious since the 1990s is that they are wound tighter and therefore are easier to blast out of the park. Major league baseball claimed before the 2021 season that steps had been taken to make baseballs less lively. Here is hoping that their efforts are effective.

The hitters do not need that help. The league has done all it can to assist them. It lowered the mounds after the Year of the Pitcher in 1968. New fan-friendly ballparks feature shorter home-run distances. The strike zone has shrunk by perhaps one-half since I pitched. The high strike is no more. Basically, pitchers must serve their pitches up on a silver platter or entice hitters to swing at balls out of the zone. And hitters often comply by hacking at high fastballs that were once strikes or at breaking balls darting outside or in the dirt. Plate discipline is practiced by far too few major league hitters today.

I cannot place all the blame on the modern player. The minor league system has undergone a transformation. Decades ago each club boasted many farm clubs in which to groom and nurture their young talent. The rules later stipulated a limit on the number of minor league organizations allowed. But aside from bonus babies who were catapulted through organizations, most players received five years of seasoning or more during which they learned the finer points of the game.

Perhaps the most pronounced difference today is the disappearance of the art of bunting. Even thirty years ago every minor league player learned how to sacrifice a runner over. Now a successful bunt should inspire a parade down Main Street. The drag bunt, which has become extinct, was especially important at one time to get runners on base in tight games. Many players of the modern era seem to have no concept of a taut battle in which just one run is sacred. They live and die instead by the home run. Players rushed to the major leagues either do not have the time or do not feel the motivation to learn their craft. They fear that they need to show something or they will be released three or four years after joining the professional ranks. And bunting is not on their priority list.

So the long ball has become the holy grail for a huge majority of hitters, even those boasting little raw power. The small ball that infused the sport with action has disappeared. The hit-and-run, sacrifice, and drag bunt have all but gone by the way of the dinosaur. One can imagine fans never again experiencing the exhilaration of watching great base stealers like Maury Willis, Lou Brock, Tim Raines, and Rickey Henderson tear up the base paths.

The science of analytics and sabermetrics has also produced radical shifts that hitters try in vain to beat rather than practice the bat control that would allow them to accept an opposite-field single or double. Pitchers are throwing harder and batters are swinging harder than ever. Split-finger fastballs and late-breaking sliders, combined with a shocking lack of discipline by bat-wielders, result in more swings-and-misses on balls in the dirt in one year than I witnessed throughout my career. Players striking out nearly two hundred times in a season have become common, whereas those in my era who fanned half that often were chastised for it. The sad result is longer and duller games.

So major league baseball and its organizations have worked to add excitement at the ballpark artificially. Loud rock and hip-hop music are blasted through the sound system between innings. Team mascots clown around and lead cheers. Restaurants and bars have been built within the stadiums. Full meals are offered when once fans were satisfied with a simple hot dog. I have no problem with any of this. I understand that the presentation needed to evolve so the game could compete as a major form of entertainment. But such diversions should add to the enjoyment of the game rather than serve as the greatest attraction in an otherwise boring event.

And I do not believe the excitement level of a ballgame need be based on the number of runs scored. A taut, 1-0 pitching duel can be thrilling—if not to the younger generations, but there is a reason for this. Such battles ran about two hours in my day. The pace was lively despite the lack of offense. In the modern era, games can last well over three hours as managers yank one pitcher after another, batters step away from the box for an inordinate amount of time, and pitchers wait thirty seconds or more between offerings to the plate. Although no one I know of has ever wanted to hurt a fellow player, if a hitter during my career had gone through all the gyrations they do today, the first pitch would have put him on the ground. Rounding the bases while showing up a pitcher would have resulted in that player sitting on his ass the next time up to the plate. I was never accused of being anything close to a headhunter, but I would not accept being shown up.

Times have indeed changed. When I arrived in the major leagues in 1961, baseball was the national pastime. When I drank myself out of the sport in 1975, it still was. In fact many believe that the game reached its peak in popularity that year, greatly because of the tremendous World Series between the Reds and the Red Sox that featured so many memorable moments, including the Carlton Fisk home run to end Game 6.

That title, "national pastime," had been earned. It was no phony boast. Baseball remained America's game for generations for a myriad of reasons, including its rich history and uniqueness. For a century its legends were revered more than their counterparts in football or basketball. Babe Ruth remains the most mythical figure in the history of American sports. And unlike those two sports, baseball used no clock. Nobody complained about the length of games because nine innings were generally completed before bedtime. Now it has become an issue, and those demanding twenty-second limits between pitches and enforcing the rule have a legitimate complaint.

That problem has contributed to pro football clearly bypassing baseball as the national pastime particularly if the definition one embraces is "the most popular game in the United States." Younger generations who crave fast-paced action reject baseball as too slow. Even passionate fans complain about the long stretches of inaction between pitches and innings that extend typical games well over three hours. And that inaction has filtered into the game itself, which has been in recent years plagued by a soaring number of strikeouts, which exceeded the number of hits for the first time in the history of the sport in 2019.

And that is a shame because major league baseball remains a great game. I am proud and thankful to have been involved in it for these many years of my adult life. My experiences have been rich and the friendships I embrace have proven to be a wonderful bonus. I received an opportunity as a player and counselor to get behind the scenes and understand the inner workings of the sport.

Among the lessons I learned first hand is that despite a drive to win, there are few secrets in baseball about players. I was surprised to discover that scouts from different teams constantly talk to each other freely about players in various organizations. They seek to find out anything and everything about personnel on other clubs.

It is quite an intriguing dance. I stayed in the same hotels as scouts during my years working with individual franchises and I also sat among them during games. You could not miss them—they were the folks holding radar guns. Scouts at the major league level evaluate opposing hitters by charting strengths and weaknesses, determining how they should be defended against based on where they are most likely to hit the ball. Any pitcher scheduled to face that club is charted as well. Velocity, late movement, and location are all noted. The scout then reports back to his team, including its pitchers, who can benefit from the data gleaned about the opposition. But what is most fascinating about the entire process is that the scouts return to their hotels after games, meet up in the bar, and openly discuss what they've seen. Discussions continue late into the night.

The same lack of secrecy played out in team management meetings I was asked to attend. I was shocked at the amount of material that flowed during these discussions. They shared gobs of information, not just about players' on-field talents and tendencies but how their family background, behavior, attitude, and any personal problems might affect performance. The thoroughness of their knowledge about opposing players in particular allowed me to gain an insight into who needed help with their personal or professional life.

During my playing career I knew about scouting reports and some of the inner workings of team management. But I had no idea just how involved and complex were the processes. I was clueless about the level of intrigue and depth of investigation involved in player evaluation. In later days I was extremely proud of the respect I had earned to even be considered a participant in some of those meetings. They trusted that what was discussed would remain confidential. I used information to find out if a player on another club was in trouble but I never shared a word that an opponent could use to aid them competitively on the field.

Despite my role in employee assistance and as a counselor that gave me a specific role to play within a major league organization, I became involved in all aspects of the team. That included the hiring and firing of coaches, managers, and trainers. I was far less involved in personnel decisions involving the minor leagues. Not all franchises make such determinations with equal seriousness. Texas and Toronto, the two teams I worked with most extensively, certainly scrutinized carefully. Some organizations hired and fired at the lower levels based more on financial concerns.

Many hires are completed without research. Among the most blatant examples are sports psychologists. I am honored that my work in that field set the wheels in motion for a trend that resulted in every team employing one. The problem is that many sports psychologists deal in straight knowledge rather than applied psychology. I have talked to some who had no clue what a professional athlete is all about. They were not giving players any help. And that is a shame. A sharp sports psychologist today can prove vital to a club.

The proof is in the pudding. Those within the game of baseball know when a player is improving. Players recognize when they are improving. The result is that athletes who study psychology are often more effective than psychologists with no sports background who have earned their doctorates. I know two former players who indeed delved into that realm and applied what they learned to help many pursuing their own baseball careers. But they do not go around philosophizing or expounding on their greatness. They let their results speak for themselves.

A similar scenario has played out regarding what are known as sabermetrics and analytics. Are experts in these fields hired by major league franchises valuable as player evaluators and strategists? Can their input be used by managers and coaches as tools in seeking to maximize performance? Yes. But is everything they sell to management beneficial? No.

Those toiling in the new science study the spin rate of pitches and the launch angle of batters. In recent years, sabermetricians have convinced those in baseball management that the ideal swing features a launch angle that results in a lot of home runs rather than one on an even plane that promotes consistent, hard contact. The strategy then becomes one that would make legendary Orioles manager Earl Weaver happy. And that is winning with pitching and three-run homers.

At one time each team had a reputation for boasting either great hitters or great pitchers. It was all based on the dynamics of the scouting system and general manager. One example was Cleveland, which featured tremendous pitching. The Yankees were known for their bashers during their dynasties. Baltimore for a short period had an ideal mix. General managers would seek managers with an understanding of his team's scouting dynamics and pick one with a reputation as an expert working with his club's weaknesses. Then the era arrived in which premier managers could handle both dynamics. Among them were Tony LaRussa, Joe Maddon, Cito Gaston, Joe Torre, and Jim Leyland.

The problem with that theory as we launch the third decade of the twenty-first century is that no team in baseball boasts the same level of pitching talent that the old Cleveland Indians had in Bob Feller, Mike Garcia, Bob Lemon, and Herb Score as well as the Indians of my era that included Steve Hargan, Sonny Siebert, Stan Williams, and Luis Tiant. My former batting practice and bullpen catcher Tom Tomsick in his book titled *Strike Three!* claimed, based on statistical data, that our rotation was the best in baseball history. Nobody can show me modern rotations that boast such depth or that of the 1971 Baltimore twenty-game-winner quartet of Jim Palmer, Dave McNally, Mike Cuellar, and Pat Dobson.

Old-school managers are smart and tough enough to use the analytic data they see as helpful and discard the rest even if it has been promoted by a general manager and his sabermetric experts. Less-experienced or -bold managers do whatever is suggested in fear of ruffling the feathers of management. But what must be known is that there is more to managing and coaching than putting statistics and research into play. There is so much more to the makeup of a player.

It all reminds me of a movie starring Brad Pitt called *Moneyball* that captured the start of the analytics movement in baseball through the travails of the 2002 Oakland Athletics. The crux of the story is that general manager Billy Beane, a former top draft pick who failed to blossom in the major leagues, angers his scouts by embracing a computerized approach to building a roster based on analytics. The film seeks to make the point that the rebuilt As thrived offensively because of their revolutionary methodology. What the writers ignored was that in reality the team finished a mediocre eighth in the American League in runs scored that season and won because of a tremendous trio of starting pitchers in Tim Hudson, Mark Mulder, and Barry Zito and lights-out closer Billy Koch. Those hurlers are conveniently never mentioned in the flick.

I have no qualms with in-depth statistical analysis that dictates where a batter is defended and how he is pitched or when a hitter should look for a slider as opposed to a changeup. Analytics certainly has its place. Has the guy at the plate made consistently hard contact against the split-finger fastball? Should the defense shift against a batter who uses the whole field because their pitcher throws a lot of off-speed stuff that results in hitters being out in front? Over the past half-century and especially lately, baseball minds have become quite interested in complex and now computerized studies to maximize competitive advantage.

But just as our societal weaknesses have taken politics to an extreme in recent years, so have the analytic forces in sports. I have met with and studied experts in disciplines such as kinesiology, engineering, and physiology on action versus reaction and other aspects of their sciences as they relate to baseball. I know managers and coaches who have done the same in an effort to better understand the human body and how it works as well as specific aspects of the game such as pitch velocity, bat speed, arm movement, hand movement, and the coilspring effect of a pitcher. They have come to conclusions that refute those made by analytics. In my work in baseball over the past four decades and in my discussions with managers and coaches it has been inevitable that they would raise the issue of management meddling in how they manage or help a player, especially lately in regard to analytics. Certainly in a few cases it may be their ego as manager or coach being infringed upon, but for the vast majority they have experienced serious interference.

I personally have seen pitchers with real talent get passed over because their fastball did not have the ideal spin rate or velocity. I have seen talented hitters denied promotion for what was perceived as weak bat speed or the poor launch angle of their swing only to find success a few years later with another club wise enough to give them a chance. Many experienced managers have recently bucked the trend and spoken out. The reply from the analytics crowd is that their critics are not knowledgeable in the sciences when the truth is that the statistical gurus are so tied up in computerized spreadsheets that they do not understand the human side of the equation. Analytics cannot judge drive and determination, the ability to rise to the occasion in a showdown sport between pitcher and batter, the focus required to track down a line drive in the gap or a hard smash in the hole.

And think about this. The incredible Greg Maddux, who could hardly throw hard enough to break a pane of glass, would never have received an opportunity today pitching under these requirements. And think of all the pitchers throughout history who would have been cast by the wayside. That would include all-time studs such as Al Oliver, Pete Rose, Tony Gwynn, and hundreds of others who did not boast the upward launch angle the modern game seems to demand. What made those players great in addition to pure talent was their attitude, mental makeup, and objective learning processes. Perhaps they would have adjusted and altered their swing to supposedly beat shifts and add power. But I contend that would have made them less-effective hitters. No team would have dared play three fielders on the right side against those hitters anyway because they used the whole field with devastating effectiveness.

The problem is that upper management has changed over the years. During previous eras, it consisted of former players or scouts. Upper management always embraced a baseball mentality. Today upper-management personnel are often educated businesspeople, many of whom have no clue about the makeup of an athlete and what is required to thrive in the sport. I am not asserting that everyone in management should necessarily be a former player. What I am contending is that what works best is a mix of minds, backgrounds, and philosophies rather than a discounting of what field managers, coaches, and scouts have to offer.

Computer analysis of hitters and pitchers can tell only part of the story. How would modern-day sabermetricians advise club management about a young Maddux? They might rail against his lack of velocity and spin rate and miss the fact that he had the balls of a burglar and could nail a dime sitting in a catcher's mitt hovered over the outside corner. He was a brain surgeon of pitching. He achieved more with less than any pitcher I have ever seen. I would pay anything to watch him artistically paint a performance. My favorite pitchers of all time were those who countered a lack of velocity and natural talent with guile such as Maddux, Gaylord Perry, and Lew Burdette. This is not to imply I do not appreciate talent. Among the other hurlers I admire are Koufax, Whitey Ford, Nolan Ryan, Bob Gibson, and Roger Clemens. Only steroid charges against the latter have prevented all five from being first-ballot Hall of Famers.

The steroid scandal turned off some fans from the sport forever. But most returned to the ballpark. I find fascinating the timeline of fan attendance and passion for baseball. From the 1940s into the 1970s, the vast knowledge of the fan base did not translate into clicking turnstiles. Some teams boasted of exceeding 1 million in attendance for a season but only the premier clubs fighting for pennants drew well. Crowds of five thousand or less were common among the weaker teams even after the advent of mostly night games provided greater opportunity for folks to attend. One result was that organizations struggled to keep their franchises alive and threatened to move them. The Indians were often reported to be on the verge of relocating during my time in Cleveland.

Franchise owners complained from the 1970s forward that the skyrocketing cost of player salaries would wreck their profit margins. So they began to cater to fans with flashy electronic scoreboards, new stadiums with less foul territory that brought patrons closer to the action, livelier baseballs, smaller dimensions, home-run derbies before All-Star Games, and a variety of inducements at the park.

But larger attendance figures do not necessarily translate into overall popularity. It is more a reflection of ballgames being promoted as entertainment happenings and the continued passion of hard-core fans. I believe it has been contended correctly that Mike Trout, the greatest player in the game today, could walk down most streets in America and not be recognized. Can one imagine Willie Mays or Mickey Mantle not being mobbed in the same scenario in the 1950s or 1960s? Families once talked about baseball in the home constantly. Parents and kids knew every player on the home team and discussed strategy. Young boys bought baseball cards, flipped them, placed them in their bicycle spokes. Now baseball cards are a big business embraced only by adults seeking to maximize their value.

And that is a shame because baseball remains better suited to statistical analysis and debate than any sport followed by fans worldwide. What might be achieved by shortening games and creating new rules that liven things up is limited. Baseball is still baseball. It will never match football or basketball as an action sport. Those marketing the game have proven unsuccessful in drumming up excitement, especially among young fans. They can be applauded for ads that feature players slamming home runs and diving for balls or showing legends like Babe Ruth and Willie Mays in an effort to educate and excite kids about the historical greatness of the game, but scheduling playoff and World Series contests that ensure young children will be in bed by the fifth inning because this maximizes primetime advertising dollars does not help.

So here is the Sam McDowell method of enticing fans. Major league baseball should launch a program at every park that enlightens and involves patrons. One example would be flashing a fun trivia question about a home-team player on the scoreboard and allowing fans to text their answers to a team official. The first fan who guesses correctly receives a voucher for a food item or souvenir.

I am saddened by the lack of interest in baseball among kids. Perhaps the fact that one rarely sees children playing pickup games these days is more a reflection of parental fear and the advent of video games that keep kids inside than a rejection of the sport itself. But what is clear is that the shunning of baseball and other physical activities outdoors has resulted in an obesity problem among children unmatched in American history.

Even amateur sports face troubling issues about which I became aware from my work with team physicians, surgeons, trainers, and rehab specialists. Among them was orthopedic surgeon and sports medicine expert Mike Ray, with whom I partnered for two decades working with former and current pro athletes. We both asked those in the field why baseball players were experiencing so many elbow and shoulder injuries at both the professional and amateur levels. For every three specialists I spoke with, I received three different answers.

But one aspect of the sad state of affairs they did agree on is that modern athletes fall woefully short in full-body conditioning. And that is because the emphasis in recent years has been to focus on and maximize talent in one sport. Those in high school and even younger eschew the notion of competing in multiple athletic activities for sheer fun and competition if they do not feel each sport can take them to the next level. As was explained to me, simply by playing different sports throughout the year, one is conditioning the entire body. The body movements in one sport exercise specific muscle groups as they work together for a common result. Those actions in football, basketball, baseball, soccer, tennis, and other sports all condition different parts of the body. As long as one continues to play a variety of sports, he or she is improving the total condition of the muscle skeleton as well as the ligaments, tendons, and connections between the bone and muscle.

The upshot is that when a young athlete conditions certain muscle groups and not others over an extended period of time, the specific movements required cause an abnormal and debilitating strain that can ruin a career. Sports medicine has done wonders in rehab and recovery but cannot produce miracles. Kids today should establish wonderful physical habits by playing pick-up and organized sports for fun and focusing on one sport only after high school.

Shallow people might complain that I am criticizing organized sports and that I am biting the hand that fed me throughout my professional life. What they do not understand is that it is my very passion for baseball and other athletic endeavors that motivates me to speak out. Only a tiny percentage of children and teenagers become professional athletes. The holy grail for amateur sports is to create a healthy, active society. That will not only strengthen professional sports but America as well. Establishing a vigorous lifestyle through well-rounded athletic experiences can carry the youth of this country through a happy and healthy adulthood.

One problem I notice in baseball today mirrors that of society. It is the follow-the-leader syndrome. It has allowed politics to creep not only into my sport but into the entire athletic spectrum, and I think that can be dangerous to the game. What I always believed, even before my baseball career, was that I am my own person. I've always refused to follow the gang. I recall in the early 1960s when all the attorneys and businessmen and union experts were soliciting votes to become the new head of the Players Association. During one team meeting, when all were allowed to speak and give their reasons to vote for them, my manager Birdie Tebbetts asked Marvin Miller very loudly if he was a Communist. Tebbetts repeated it later in the clubhouse. As Miller, who later led the charge for player freedom, mentioned in his book, I was the only player who voted for him. It is the same in life and society. The majority of people in gangs, organizations, unions go along with whatever the leaders decide. I reject that gang mentality. A minority of people actually think through and decide what is best for themselves, their country, or their organization. It is seen on all sides of politics today.

20

SUDDEN SAM,
MAYDAY MALONE,
AND A NEW BRIDE

I s it possible to be more famous as somebody else than yourself? It certainly was for me in the 1980s.

While I was quite anonymously launching my recovery from addiction and starting my new life, a character in a soon-to-be-well-known sitcom was beginning to entertain millions. The sitcom was *Cheers*, and his name was Sam "Mayday" Malone. He was played superbly by Ted Danson, who received eleven nominations for outstanding lead character in a comedy series, won twice for his role as a tremendously talented major league pitcher whose career had been hampered then cut short by alcoholism. Sound familiar? It should—his character was based on me.

I would have loved the show without that link. I found it highly enjoyable. I might not have even known about my relation to the Malone character had a Cleveland attorney friend familiar with the show not informed me that its writers knew my story and were actually fans of Sam McDowell, which inspired the connection. His fictional recovery coincided chronologically with my real one.

There were, of course, differences between us. I did not run a bar in Boston, and he had been a relief pitcher. Another was that Mayday never married (though he twice got close with Diane). He was a woman-chasing bachelor. I had already been wed twice when *Cheers* ended its highly decorated run in 1993. And I was open to another long-term relationship. I simply had not found the love of my life. Then it happened. The year was 1998.

The seeds of the story were planted a decade earlier when I met Toronto Blue Jays pitcher Todd Stottlemyre, whose quite talented father Mel matched up against me often on the mound as ace of the Yankees staff in the 1960s. Todd and I became close friends. Meanwhile, my son Tim and I befriended a golf pro named Greg Gagliano, who worked at the Landsbrook Club in Palm Harbor, Florida. Tim and I, as well as my girlfriend at the time, all owned homes at the Tarpon Woods Country Club, which was across the street from Landsbrook, where we all played often.

Eventually Todd and Greg hatched a plan to build their own championship golf course. Todd sought investors, including friends such as me and his father. The result was the Diamond Players Club in Clermont. Gagliano also acquired management contracts with two other golf courses that had been failing. He became so busy that he called on me to help manage his clubs in 1998. It was an inviting proposal. I sold all my investments in Tarpon Woods and purchased a home in Clermont, just six blocks between both the Diamond Players Club and the Legends Golf Course.

It was a life-changing move. But commuting from Pittsburgh to Florida had become a grind so shifting full time to the Sunshine State proved beneficial personally and professionally. I continued to visit relatives in Pittsburgh three or four times a year and enjoyed invitations from the Pirates for their Christmas Dinner for the Alumni and annual charity golf tournament. I relished opportunities to visit with former player friends there. But living in Florida allowed me to start a more relaxing career. Even so I continued to work for BAT—my formal retirement had not begun yet.

Not that I ever really retired. I have not been one to gain satisfaction wiling the hours away in a rocking chair. I continued to keep my eyes and ears open not so much for money-making ventures but to find new ways to help people. Such a possibility arose when I met orthopedic surgeon Mike Ray during one of my many flights back and forth between Pittsburgh and Clermont. He was a sports-medicine specialist who had not only treated Olympians and triathletes but had helped save the careers of professional football and baseball players. He had also worked to repair the knees, shoulders, hips, and elbows of retired athletes. A humble man, he had done so without seeking publicity.

Ray expressed a tremendous interest in my work with BAT. We decided to seek out ways as a team to help retired athletes struggling to make ends meet and who had seriously abused their bodies in action. We arrived at the idea of flying those who did not have an orthopedic specialist to Clermont for free help funded by BAT. I approached BAT with the idea and received an enthusiastic thumbs-up. The result was that Ray selflessly helped many retired athletes who had no insurance and at no cost to them.

In 2001 he began studying stem cell therapy, which had been embraced in other parts of the world and had attracted a wide variety of celebrities dealing with pain management. While medical professionals in other countries had been using and perfecting it for more than three decades, the United States had fallen behind. Ray and I studied papers and spoke often about it over the next two years.

The simple definition of stem cell therapy is that it is a system that helps bodies heal themselves. When we're born and while a child we have trillions of stem cells helping us grow tissue, helping us fix or heal certain injuries. As we grow older our stem cells dwindle to the point that when we are in our fifties and beyond we have comparatively few. There are many different types of stem cells that are found in many areas of the body, including fatty tissue and bone marrow. Each has different qualities for different purposes.

Stem cell therapy remained banned in the United States largely because of the control of big pharmaceutical companies, but we continued to study its benefits with great interest. It was finally opened up in America and even aided a former athlete known as Sudden Sam, who for about a quarter century had no meniscus in either knee. Since the pain was minimal I lived through it. But in 2017 I twisted my knee stumbling on a sprinkler on the golf course. The pain was excruciating.

I had been advised by doctors that eventually I would require a knee replacement so I asked Ray about stem cells. He asked me drive to his practice in Naples. There he injected stem cells in my knee. Two weeks later the pain was gone. I was blown away but still skeptical because during my baseball career, shots of lidocaine eliminated pain for several hours but the pain then returned. European research papers about stem cell treatments claimed that healing could last from a few years to permanently but it still had to be proven to me.

Soon I received another painful opportunity. I tore my right shoulder rotator cuff moving furniture in my home in 2018. I could not move it without agony. I wasted no time after the original diagnosis to contact Ray, who by that time was using exosomes, the powerful healing properties of stem cells. He injected exosomes in my shoulder, and four days later the pain had completely disappeared. An MRI did not show any evidence of the tear three weeks later. I quickly recommended stem cell therapy to my wife Eva, who was suffering from serious arthritis in her hands and a strained shoulder ligament. She received exosomes shots in her shoulder and intravenously in her arm for the arthritis. By the time we returned home from our three-and-a-half hour drive, her pain was gone. I am now sold on exosomes.

One can only imagine just how beneficial such treatment could be for retired athletes, especially football players, whose physical issues later in life have been well-documented. Ray and I have in recent years begun work with various

companies to create a program to help former athletes. I was indeed particularly shocked while attending a convention of retired NFL players. About three
thousand were in attendance and I would estimate that three-fourths of them
had serious problems walking. We have since become involved and hope to
continue helping. Why should these men live out their lives as cripples when
they can be healed?

One problem is that stem cell therapy in the United States is so new that
most medical personnel are unfamiliar with how it works despite the fact that
Europeans have benefitted from the results for decades. My primary physician
originally thought it was a myth then dismissed research when I showed it to
him. Because I am still involved with many of the medical professions, I speak
with those in different disciplines. And only perhaps one in twenty recognize
the therapy. All they need is an open mind and a bit of education. My pulmon-
ologist saw the results of my different breathing tests and inhalation therapy. He
was sold and is now part of our formal studies.

Positive results with autism, Parkinson's, chronic obstructive pulmonary
disease, and arthritis are finally receiving attention from the medical profession. But it is a slow process. The retirement village in which I currently live is
a prime example. Neither the homeowners nor the medical professionals here
have any clue about stem cells—the helpful ones and the not so helpful ones—
and their benefits.

My move to Florida proved eventful beyond my introduction to stem cell
therapy. I gained a wonderful companion in my personal life. The monumental moment that brought me love would not have happened had GPS been in
existence in 1998. I was asked that year to present an award to Carmen Bush,
wife of then-Florida governor Jeb Bush, for all her work with teenagers on drug
prevention. The event was scheduled for Dr. Phillips High School in Orlando.
I needed to ask for directions along the way. In such situations I always pick a
large shopping center so if one person does not know I can always ask another.

I spotted a K-mart with plenty of vehicles in front and I noticed a woman
getting out of a yellow sports car. A vision of loveliness. Why not get directions
and meet a beautiful blonde at the same time, right? It became obvious that she
could not speak English very well so since I had a bit of time to kill I asked her to
join me for a cup of coffee. She paused for a bit, then agreed. After learning her
name was Eva and that she was Slovakian, I asked her to meet me at my country
club at nine o'clock after I returned from the banquet. Another yes.

But did she mean it? I repeatedly called the country club chef from the event
to find out if she had arrived. The answer every time was no. I assumed she'd
had second thoughts and cancelled. After all, a quick cup of coffee near K-mart

does not exactly constitute a lengthy introduction. I made one last call. Bingo! She was there. We enjoyed our time together and began dating. I found her fascinating. I learned that she once served as director of entertainment for the Slovakian government, a connection that later came in handy when we visited her native land and family.

Among the first idiosyncrasies I noticed was that no matter how high-class the restaurant we visited in Orlando and central Florida, she would always order shrimp cocktail and salad. I finally asked her why and she explained to me that those were the only two items on the menu she could decipher in English. But she studied the language, adding it to the list she spoke fluently that already included Slovakian, Russian, Polish, and Czech. She could also speak but not read German.

Eventually I began thinking about marriage. But I hesitated. The idea brought back haunting memories. Alcoholism wrecked my first one and my second lasted but nine months. I felt fortunate to have met and dated several wonderful women since then but my past seemed to have precluded the notion of tying another knot.

I fell in love with Eva and as we grew more involved, the thought of marriage became a pleasant one. I shared with her neither my worries nor hopefulness. I felt the need to clear my mind. It would not have been fair for me to bring my baggage along in our relationship. After all, being in a good recovery that had already lasted nearly two decades guaranteed nothing. I wanted to ensure that I was ready for my first proper, caring, and loving marriage. My fears could best be described as paranoia.

Time and Eva healed that mental wound. After a couple years of dating I decided to pop the question. She was special and I wanted the moment to be special. I planned to ask her for her hand on her birthday. My secretary made wonderful plans. She invited Eva's friends—some who flew in from Slovakia and whom she had not seen in years—for a party at the country club restaurant. The event was attended by about thirty-five people. Eva and I sat in the middle of a long table. We began the festivities with a fine meal. Then it was time for dessert. Little did she know that her engagement ring had been planted in a huge cake baked by our chef and that soon I would ask her to marry me.

The cake was ready. I was ready. The chef gave me a signal. I tapped Eva on the shoulder and she turned to me. "Honey, I'd like to ask you something," I said. She turned away and continued her conversation with friends. I tried to ask her again and she turned away again. So I waved to the chef. He brought the cake over to the table so she could not miss it. No dice. She kept talking with her friends. What she eventually could not miss was the large, shiny diamond ring resting in between layers of cake. The room fell silent. Everyone but me believed what they'd attended was simply a birthday party.

A look of shock fell over Eva. "What are you telling?" she blurted out. "I'm asking you to marry me," I replied. More silence as she came to grips with the enormity of the event. She began to cry. In between tears she said, "Yes!" Bedlam erupted throughout the restaurant. An occasion to remember forever.

One might be shocked to learn that I had never revealed my baseball career to Eva. She did not become aware of it until years later when we flew to Pittsburgh for the annual Pirates Christmas party. While I was in the bathroom, Ginger Briles, wife of fine pitcher Nelson Briles, turned to Eva and asked, "Do you know who you're married to?" She replied quizzically, "Yes . . . Sam." Ginger said, "No, you're married to one of the great pitchers in baseball." All she had known after hearing me take calls in the wee hours of the morning was that I was a counselor. That night and several thereafter she peppered me with questions about baseball. I had never unpacked my trophy collection or awards from my time in the sport. They'd been all stuck in the garage for about eighteen years and I just never got around to taking everything out to dust and clean.

Eva eventually became keen to my first career. I introduced her to many former Indians players during an event in Cleveland. They were intrigued by her accent. Among them were my former pitching mates Gary Bell and Louie Tiant. They wanted to know if Eva and I ever argued. "I don't know," I replied. "I don't understand Slovakian and she doesn't understand English."

One might wonder why during all those years with Eva I did not reveal that I was once a famous athlete. Two factors entered into the equation. The first was that as part of my recovery I had to understand that the past had passed. I was a recovering alcoholic only, not a former ballplayer. I took my revival as a person so seriously that I truly let go of my previous career. I became so involved with counseling that it was no longer important. I never brought it up—not to Eva or anyone else unless they gained that knowledge on their own and inquired.

The subject of my baseball career arose when friends or neighbors discovered it on their own. But that was rare. To them I was just one of the boys and that is the way I liked it. I wanted them to appreciate me for me, not my uniform. As for Eva, why would she care? That was my mindset. I thought a few times about telling her but I figured as a Slovakian it would mean nothing to her.

Anyway, I introduced her family to the sport when we visited. They were not the only folks there to learn about the game. Rawlings donated $10,000 of equipment and balls for me to put on clinics in Slovakia. One was held in an open field in front of the old Communist headquarters building. There were no baseball diamonds—just soccer fields. But they had to suffice.

Eva did more than suffice as a wife. I had married a gem. She was indeed born under Communist rule in Czechoslovakia in 1958. The nation remained under a repressive regime until 1987—an experiment with greater freedom under progressive leader Alexander Dubcek in 1968 was brutally quashed by the Russian army. She arrived in America in the early 1990s in what was intended to be a three-month stay. She enjoyed her stay so much she decided to stick around a bit longer and procure a work visa. But after we'd met and had been dating for a while she secured a permanent visitor visa. A year later we were wed—quite a shock for her given that I had repeated over and over to her that I would never marry again. Famous last words.

Eva began the rigorous process of gaining United States citizenship in 2001. It required background searches including family history as well as education in American history and the English language. She finally earned citizenship in 2008 after a seven-year period she considers well worth the struggle.

She has come a long way. And she has taken me a long way. I acquired new knowledge and interests through her background. Her upbringing in a Communist country has led to many spirited conversations and a thirst for understanding that filled me with respect for her. I am amazed at the courage and strength it took for her to move to a foreign land without speaking the language, having no protection from family and friends. I know I could never have done that.

I have become quite the expert on European governments, particularly from the old Eastern bloc. What I learned from Eva greatly differed from the lessons taught in history class. It was a thrill for me to travel to Europe to visit her family members throughout Slovakia and the Czech Republic as well as other countries in that area of the world. They even threw a birthday bash for me inside the old Communist Party headquarters in the center of Slovakia. My opportunity to soak in many of the World War II sites proved eye opening and emotional. Among them was Auschwitz, the deadliest killing factory of the Holocaust. I felt sickened but also enlightened listening to Eva's family members and neighbors talk about their experiences during the war and beyond. It must be noted that Eastern Europe slid right from the horrors of the war into the horrors of Russian oppression and stifled freedom.

Her growth as a person and an American has inspired me. She formed her own cleaning business and acquired the contracts of many stores in Florida. My children have embraced her and we have even become friends with Carol and her husband. We spend time with them when we visit Pittsburgh where my kids, their families, and some of my relatives still live. Eva and I travel throughout the United States and I find it admirable how she excitedly learns about the land and history of her adopted nation. What I once took for granted about living in America I have gained greater appreciation for because of Eva. She points out facts about our country that I had forgotten.

Oh, and her cooking! I can hardly imagine that she rarely cooked in her life before we met. She has blossomed into an incredible cook and baker. Wherever we have lived, the neighbors quickly discovered her expertise and demanded one of her masterpieces, particularly her specialty, an Irish wedding cake that requires eight hours of baking time. Folks fall over themselves scrambling for a slice.

It all added up. I was a late bloomer. But now that I had blossomed I yearned to maximize my potential as a person and enjoy life to the fullest. One more major weakness remained. It was time to kick a habit that had gripped me since before I stepped onto a professional ball field.

21

VICES BAD AND GOOD

If a new year is supposed to inspire resolutions, a new millennium should motivate major declarations. And I made one when the calendar turned not just to another century but to the year 2000 (though it has been suggested that the millennium actually began in 2001). I had decided to stop smoking.

Granted, I got scared into it more than anything else. I learned for the first time during a visit to my cardiologist late one morning that I had a heart problem. It was suggested quite strongly that I stop puffing down cigarettes, a habit I started at age sixteen and that once peaked at three-and-a-half packs a day. The doctor did not indicate that smoking had damaged my heart or even contributed to the problem but emphasized that it could slow and even negate all efforts to return it to health.

My issue was atrial fibrillation, a rapid and irregular heartbeat. Doctors attempted everything from shocking my heart directly to working their way through the arteries in my leg to the heart to determine the possible benefits of cardiac ablation, a procedure that scars tissue in the heart to block abnormal electrical signals and restore a healthy rhythm. I was left with a therapeutic plan of medication and constant monitoring. The doctor determined that even a pacemaker or heart stimulator would not produce the desired results.

My recovery from alcoholism had apparently not rid me of an inclination to deny all personal problems. When it came to smoking cigarettes, I sought information that refuted claims that my habit endangered any opportunity to strengthen my heart. I was an addict and I continued to justify my desire to smoke.

But I was not the same person who years earlier would have clenched his teeth and refused to change. Not only had I matured as a man, I boasted a powerful ally. Her name was Eva. I sat down with my wife after pondering my health for a few days and discussed with her the possibility of quitting. I understood that nicotine was a very seductive chemical and that kicking the habit would be tough. I wanted us to do it together—she was a smoker as well. I figured we could give each other the strength to rid ourselves of our nasty craving. So we began to look into a variety of programs, products, and plans. We were initially discouraged. I saw virtually nothing but ineffective money makers.

Then one morning in dawned on me. The epiphany arrived as I shaved and it caused me to laugh. Eva looked at me like I had six heads. So I told her that the answer to my smoking problem was internal, not external. I needed no plan. I had myself. The man who had learned to beat the demon alcoholism could use the same strategy to defeat cigarette addiction.

Soon I was working with Eva to prepare for the games we needed to play to win the battle. I knew that my body would demand the feelings I got from nicotine such as energy, stimulation, relaxation, alertness, and a satisfaction similar to that of making love to my wife. No exaggeration. After four decades of smoking, I was really hooked.

I had to quit cold turkey but not immediately. I needed five days to wean off. So I continued to smoke for five days, but on each of them I would cut the cigarettes with a scissors to draw in less. My last day in the process was a Friday. At around 11:15 p.m. Eva asked me if I was coming to bed. I said no. I had forty-five minutes left to smoke and I was going to use every second. I almost did. I put the last one out at 11:55. That is how addicts act.

As the sinister demands of our bodies and minds reared their ugly heads and seemed overwhelming, we would discuss our feelings. I would explain to Eva based on my experiences in recovery what was happening and how we needed to defend against it to continue with our daily and nightly activities. Once we took the time to think about and understand the effect quitting was having on our bodies and minds, we could handle the situation. We gave each other support and beat it. Neither of us has puffed on a cigarette for twenty-one years. We still experienced urges. But with each passing day they dissipated a bit more. And since we understood that the demands of nicotine addiction can be evil and what forms they could take, we could more easily defeat them.

I have been asked what the learned, experienced Sam would tell Sam the child if time travel allowed him to return to the old homestead in Pittsburgh sixty or seventy years ago. The answer is easy. I would not say anything specifically. I would work to improve his self-esteem because that was the core problem that played a devastating role in his addiction. I believe the educational system in America has since let its children down regarding strengthening self-image. There was an emphasis on building self-esteem in our classrooms in the 1960s and 1970s that was left behind in the decades to follow as irrelevant to curriculum. Yet research clearly shows that one of the greatest tools to prevent poor behavior and issues in adulthood, including addiction and abuse, is boosting self-image during youth.

Yet despite the fog I lived in as a kid and young adult, as well as my narcissism and other negative personality traits, all of which resulted in my addiction and an inability to maximize my potential as a person and pitcher, I never look back in regret. Never. I do not agonize. This shocks some people who know about the talent I possessed, the results of my career, and what could have been. Indeed it has been claimed that I could have been another Sandy Koufax. But negative reminiscing is a reflection for fools. One must always try to look ahead with a positive mindset. It is a truism that we cannot change the past, we can only learn from it. That is what I have tried to do. I have used my experiences to help others and plan to continue in those endeavors despite having retired from counseling. That is the motivation for this autobiography.

In the meantime I enjoy my hobbies, some of which helped me through the darkest days and continue to provide peace of mind and a sense of accomplishment. Among the most important is painting. I enjoyed drawing pictures when I was six to ten years old and that passion has continued throughout my life. My medium is acrylics. After signing my first baseball contract, I took a three-year correspondence course with the Famous Artists School. My love for painting has remained with me ever since.

I recall the *Sports Illustrated* article that featured me in 1970 and listed my hobbies, including painting, collecting guns, constructing model boats inside bottles, selling organic cosmetics, training German shepherds, as well as running a family pool hall. Critics claimed that the variety of activities, all of which had nothing to do with baseball, indicated that I was a man without direction. But writer Pat Jordan observed that several of those pursuits could be worked at in solitude and isolation, away from the judgmental eyes of others.

He was right. And the cynics were wrong. My motivation for embarking on a variety of diversions was based on interests in those pastimes and a desire I had that my entire existence be well rounded. Baseball had never been my driving force, my primary focus in life. Later in my career and for several years after I could not concentrate on anything through my alcoholic haze. But the deep desire to expand my horizons, to quench my thirst for knowledge, to learn and grow, never left me. The difference after my recovery was that a clear mind and a healthier body allowed me to pursue and achieve those goals.

During my career many people did not understand. They grew more critical as I aged and it became apparent to them that I would never maximize my pitching potential. They could not fathom in that era, nor could they have known, that personal problems and not my hobbies were holding me back. I annoyed fans and folks inside the game who believed I treated those diversions with the same reverence as I did my pitching. What they did not realize was that I put my heart and soul into one and all. I worked hard at my craft. Why else would I have been so angry at those who handcuffed me and prevented me from learning the science of pitching?

But I was not about to quit all my other interests to focus solely on baseball. When one lives for challenges, as I did, he can place all his energy in each one individually. My varied positive diversions did not weaken my concentration and effort on the mound. At one point I even took up photography and rather than sending my shots away I developed them myself. It was all part and parcel of my escapism. I could float on any cloud of whatever I was doing and for that period of time not be forced to deal with the real world. Anyway, the last thing I needed in 1970 was more time to drink.

It was sobriety that turned my life around and allowed me to re-engage in all my passions, including those that were handed down. Among them was home improvement, a hobby I picked up from my father. I do not boast the skill to construct at the level of my father but I do enjoy renovation and restoration. I am proud to have helped build our residence in Monroeville and am still capable of fixing things that break around our Florida home, just like my dad would have done. I appreciated my father and tried to embrace the same motivations. I always have. When I was a kid and given the rare opportunity to spend a little money, I often purchased model planes, boats, or cars. They were comparatively simple, plastic models. And though I could not enjoy my hobbies as other kids did because my alcoholic personality prevented me from experiencing genuine joy, I did receive a sense of satisfaction putting those models together.

Later in life, the fun was in building my ships in bottles. Upon finishing my work I would give or throw them away, though a few years ago I was offered $1,000 for one of my ships. I then began buying a semi-kit for $400, spending several months constructing it, then selling it. It has worked out well but I do not receive what my time and effort are worth. I am driven by self-satisfaction. The money is of no consequence. I've built probably seven or eight USS *Constitutions* of all sizes. A friend offered me $4,000 for one of them but I could not take his money. I gave it to him, and he had been building ships himself for many years. I also showed him how to wire ships using LED micro lights and transistors and transformers so that if you cut the power, the LEDs flicker as the candlelight did back in the days of those old ships. Pretty cool.

My motivation is not only relaxation or calmness. I also seek to gain knowledge, pride, and pleasure. I still purchase and soak in educational programs. Among these is a virtual workshop on new research and data about addiction and recovery. I also read about budding therapeutic approaches. Some of them are worthless. They simply patronize the addicted to make money. But I do like to keep up even though I am retired from counseling.

That retirement brought Eva and me to the Villages of Hadley in 2013. I had always been impressed by the cleanliness and beauty of this large Florida community so we moved in. Its medical facilities are important as well—heck, I am now seventy-eight years old. And though I rarely look back on my baseball career, I need no reminders from myself. The folks here remember my playing days quite well and regale me with their own baseball stories at a supermarket or restaurant. Some of them know more about the modern game than I do.

And that is fine because I am happy, an emotion foreign to me most of my life. I feel a strong sense of self-esteem, achievement, contentment. My recovery has allowed me to give of myself to colleagues and family. I can be a good friend, a good father, a good husband. I am unaffected by the past horrors in my personal and professional lives, yet use what I learned from them to help others.

I am thankful for those who have loved and cared about me. They supported me through my darkest days. Life is a journey, and mine at one time was stormier than most. But now I sail in peaceful waters. It feels wonderful.

INDEX

ABOUT THE AUTHORS

Sam McDowell was a six-time American League All-Star pitcher whose career was derailed by alcoholism. After hitting rock bottom in 1980 he launched his recovery and studied psychology, sports psychology, and counseling. He has worked as an addiction counselor in major league baseball for more than forty years.

Martin Gitlin has won more than forty-five awards as a sportswriter, including first place for general excellence from the Associated Press for his coverage of the World Series. He is the author of more than two hundred books on a variety of subjects including many about baseball.